I LOVE YOU
ALL THE NUMBERS

A Carer's Story

ESCHANI TAYLOR

BALBOA.PRESS
A DIVISION OF HAY HOUSE

ACKNOWLEDGEMENTS

An enormous thank you goes to my darling Geoffrey. You shared with me the best of both our lives as well as my most challenging times caring for you. Thank you to my family, Geoffrey's family and my soul-family, all of whom gave continuous love as well as energetic, emotional, physical and mental support. A special thank you to Tamara. Without your initial 'Insights' editing, I couldn't have finished this book. For my friends who were there for me, Lyn and Paul and too many others to mention who were either supportive over the phone or over a coffee, a huge thank you. I am grateful also for the support from the team at Balboa Press.

INTRODUCTION

9.30 p.m.:

"What's in the diary for tomorrow?"

"You've got a doctor's appointment at nine thirty in the morning, that's all"

"OK."

"Goodnight, darling."

"Goodnight."

5.30 a.m.:

"What's on today?"

"You've got a doctor's appointment at nine thirty this morning, that's all."

"Well, I'd better get up then. C'mon! Come on, or we won't have enough time!"

Oh my God, I thought. Of course it was going to take us nearly four hours to get ready and get to his appointment—*not*! But I got up, and so the day began, because to argue or to attempt to reason with him was futile. He had dementia. You see?

It had only been a few months since his diagnosis, and I could already see the slow, very slow, but regular deterioration. He thought that he was fine and didn't notice all the little things that I had to try, every day, to be enormously patient about.

When Geoffrey was first diagnosed with dementia, it had been eighteen months since his aortic valve replacement surgery (open-heart surgery), which had been a difficult journey of almost six weeks in hospital, then rehabilitation, then back to hospital with complications from his medications, and more. Those six weeks were undeniably stressful, to say the least. In fact, I could write a whole book based upon just those six weeks … but I digress. Once Geoffrey was finally home, still in a weakened state, it was clear that his cognitive function was not what it used to be. I was patient. I thought he'd come good after a time. I was wrong.

Something that I wish to explain here, before you read any further, is that I have written this narrative from my perspective only. Other people may find dealing with someone who has dementia to be entirely different. In actual fact, there will be differences for others, and sometimes the experiences I share will be exactly the same. In many ways, dementia or no dementia, there are similarities in carers' perspectives no matter who you might be caring for and whatever brain dysfunction is present. *Dementia* is a broad label that encompasses a spectrum of incapacities and changes.

Geoffrey and I worked in personal growth education for a great many years, and I have lived consciously with a spiritual approach. Throughout the years, we have explained viewing the world from your perspective in the following way:

> Imagine a building brick standing upon its end in the middle of a room. What do you see? Depending upon where you are in the room, you will see only one aspect or perspective of that brick. You might see a totally flat solid side, a corner, or you might be able to see through the holes in the brick all the way to the other side of

the room. You might see any perspective in between the two opposites and from varying heights based upon your vertical position as well. What is true is that you can only see what you can see, based upon where you are around the brick—your perspective. You can argue your view against others who are seeing a totally different perspective and try to convince them that your perspective is the right one simply because that is what you can see. Until you move towards someone else's place in the room, you will be unable to see the brick from that perspective. Remaining where you are and blatantly insisting that your perspective is the right perspective means that you can never understand there is more than one way to view the brick.

To be fair, there is no *correct* perspective; there is only the perspective we choose to see or experience. If you remain inflexible in life and never shift yourself in order to see things from another perspective, your life will be narrow and limited.

Welcome to my perspective!

The signs used to compile this list are published by the American Academy of Family Physicians (AAFP) in the journal *American Family Physician*.

Possible symptoms of dementia:

- **Recent memory loss** – a sign of this might be asking the same question repeatedly.
- **Difficulty completing familiar tasks** – for example, making a drink or cooking a meal.
- **Problems communicating** – difficulty with language; forgetting simple words or using the wrong ones.
- **Disorientation** – getting lost on a previously familiar street, for example.
- **Problems with abstract thinking** – for instance, dealing with money.
- **Misplacing things** – forgetting the location of everyday items such as keys, or wallets, for example.
- **Mood changes** – sudden and unexplained changes in outlook or disposition.
- **Personality changes** – perhaps becoming irritable, suspicious or fearful.
- **Loss of initiative** – showing less interest in starting something or going somewhere.

As the patient ages, late-stage dementia symptoms tend to worsen.

So my research told me these things. Nothing explains what it's going to be like or how to live with it. I went searching, and the Alzheimer's Australia website initially yielded very little beyond the basics facts which I already knew. What I was actually looking for was some help, some support—emotional support. I had never in my life felt so alone. It was as if that one word collided with my world, and it was going to crumble everything.

My comfortable world was wonderful. Geoffrey and I had been together for over twenty-four years, and we had spent all day every day together for the great majority of those years. We were best friends, business partners, buddies, mates, lovers, and devoted equals. Both coming from previous long-term marriages, we brought out the best in each other.

There had been some difficulties in the beginning—the your-kids-my-kids sort of things, not to mention a sorting out of all the finances. But Geoffrey's children were grown and mine were teenagers. Eventually, the dust settled, and all was well. In fact, we quickly grew to have great relationships with not only all the children but also both of our ex-partners.

At the time of Geoffrey's diagnosis, though, all our family and friends were far away. We'd moved twelve months earlier from Melbourne to the Gold Coast. We moved for the lifestyle and the better weather. Queensland's Gold Coast is a fantastic place to retire to. We were living ten minutes from the beach, ten minutes from the hinterland, shops only eight hundred metres away, and a large shopping centre one kilometre away. Our dream home, although not fancy, was well-built, spacious, and had everything we needed, including spare rooms for visiting family or friends, a beautiful pool, and a delightful aspect over bushland and golf course.

In Melbourne, we had worked together for over twenty-four years running a personal growth and self-development company. We ran classes, courses, workshops, and retreats offering a holistic, metaphysical perspective. In more recent years, we had given up any corporate work and focussed on private clients. Many of these beautiful people had become friends as well as clients, and now we were, of course, far away from this support network too.

We had intended, when we moved north, to return to Melbourne three or four times a year for a week or so to continue with regular classes for our main mastery class and also support our small mentor groups with a session each. Although personally, we would take no payment from the business for this, we would catch up with family and friends as well as keep the business going and look after our loyal clients. Plus, I loved my work, and just because it was no longer full-time, I loved it no less.

Tamara, my eldest daughter, was still working part-time for us in the business, keeping things ticking over, looking after accounts, tending to the social media, and sorting the schedules for our Melbourne trips. I thought it all sounded perfect and would be easy to do, as well as giving us a good lifestyle. And for our first year living in Queensland, it worked out very well. I did notice that I had to take on more and more as Geoffrey was able to contribute less than he used to, but I still thought he would get better. Maybe the evidence was there and I was in denial; I don't know.

When the *dementia* word hit me, a myriad of questions about the future ran through my mind. Would I be able to look after him? How long could I do this? How would we manage financially? What would I do if/when I couldn't manage to look after him or if/when he no longer remembered who I was? Where could he go? How do I look into this? What would happen with our Melbourne trips? How could I still run our regular classes that I loved doing in Melbourne? What about the house? Would I have to sell it? What would I do for money? Who could possibly help me? The scenarios ran wildly through my mind.

Geoffrey was on an aged pension, and I applied for and received a carer's pension. We had limited funds in reserve. My mind went to all sorts of scary possibilities. I felt panicked, sad, scared, and alone. I just wanted to cry and cry. It wasn't fair—just wasn't fair at all.

INSIGHT - ONE

Having been a personal growth/self-empowerment educator for twenty-five years, I had taught many skills, tools, and techniques to help others improve their day-to-day lives and gain strength in times of stress. Taking responsibility for what we think and what we feel is something that is not usually considered in our society, as we tend to blame others for our circumstances. You only need to turn on any of the current affairs programs to see our "steeped in blame" society at work.

In our Western society, people live their lives falling from one drama to another, entangling themselves in a myriad of feelings whilst continually blaming either their current situation or the words or behaviours of others. There is no personal responsibility at all for how they feel. In fact, many people actually believe that they have no way at all to control how they feel. They believe that their happiness and peace of mind depends entirely upon external circumstances being OK. This means that when something difficult occurs in their life, they are powerless to change how they feel. Anger and misery surely follow, and an unhappy life is created.

From a metaphysical and personal-growth aspect, I know that I am responsible for my feelings. No one feels my feelings except me. In fact, I can choose how I feel.

My philosophy is empowering. I can choose to stay unhappy, or I can choose to see the *is-ness* of a situation and let how it is be OK. Often, when I feel extremely overwhelmed by a feeling, this is not quite so easy to do. I remind myself that, no matter what occurs, I am OK. I am always looked after. I trust in a higher power, and I know that all my experiences make me stronger. I always look for my options. I ask myself questions: What possibilities are there? What do I need to understand in order to feel OK? What or where is another viewpoint? What is another perspective of the brick? There are many different questions which can help me regain my balance.

I needed to do some research, and fast—before I disappeared into the quicksand of self-pity. *Okay, Mr Google*, I thought. *Here I come.*

I think because I was anxious, confused, and sad, I found very little that felt like real support or help the first time I went searching. I looked for support groups on the Gold Coast and initially found nothing. Armed with only a little information, I steeled myself for the upcoming phone calls to the family.

How do you tell your stepchildren, albeit grown women, that their daddy has dementia? Because I was still emotional about it all, it was difficult not to cry when I spoke to them. I didn't want to worry them, but I didn't want to sugar-coat it either. I did suggest to Geoffrey's youngest daughter, who lived in New Zealand, that she might not want to leave it too long before she visited her dad, as it was guesswork as to how quickly or slowly he might deteriorate. I didn't want her to miss him, so to speak.

I got through all the family phone calls and sent an open and honest email to all our friends in Melbourne letting them know what was going on. This is part of what I wrote. I have removed some of the personal references:

> Most of you have seen the slight deterioration of Geoffrey's cognitive function during our last trip back to Melbourne. You've probably noticed that it takes him even longer to think of words, or he's been extra quiet, or maybe not quite answering the exact question that you asked …
>
> He's been diagnosed with vascular dementia. In short, his brain is deteriorating. There is no cure. For those thinking natural remedies—yes, he's on everything there is that might help. His vitamin D levels are up, and his B12 is excellent. We are eating healthy food, etc., and he's taking all his other supplements.
>
> The prognosis is not exciting, with the doctor saying to expect one to two years before I will no longer be able to care for him at home.
>
> Right now, he has many "good" days—more so than bad days … On the good days, you wouldn't notice at all that anything is wrong, as he seems very normal. He just has "forgetting" times. Then there are things that he says that are "old thoughts or happenings". He gets grumpy easily, and having a common-sense

discussion or being logical with him is useless, and he just gets cross.

He will listen to an old CD of our "personal empowerment" work and then get very excited about something that the mentor group just *has* to know or they should be working with—and it is as if he has just discovered it. It makes him happy and makes him feel useful.

On the bright side, he has no idea that he is getting worse. He knows that his memory is not what it was but doesn't realise that he's asked me the same question about something three times. (I am grateful at this stage that it's *only* three times.)

He feels he is getting better physically (he's not) and that he is just fine and that his world is good.

I have to have *lots* of patience, and I have lots to work on in myself. It is bringing up a great deal for me, because in essence, I am slowly but surely losing my darling.

It also means that our arrangement of coming down to Melbourne to work for a week every three months has a very limited time left. We'll just see how we go with that.

I am continuing with my chorus and my quartet, but moving forward, I'll need him to have someone here regularly so that I can have a life—which I *have to* do for me! I am sure there are organisations I can get help from with that; I just haven't found them yet.

In that vein, though, I intend to still go to choral competition in Wollongong in mid-May, but I don't know how he will be then—and he very well might still be mostly OK, but I'd hate him to struggle cos I wasn't here. As I haven't set any help here yet and so have no one to ask from up here, is there anyone who would like to come up for a week (or more) to have a holiday? You'd probably only need to do the meals— breakfast and dinner, cos he can do his own lunch if stuff is left for him, so you wouldn't need to be here all the time … but over those four days that I'm away, I would have peace of mind knowing he wasn't alone all the time. You could use our car too. He would only know that you are coming up for a rest/holiday, so it's for *you*, not him.

I know it's a big ask, as right now, I doubt that I'm able to help with airfares or anything. Please know that I love you all and appreciate your love and support in whatever packages you give it (i.e. a loving text goes a long way, thanks xxx).

Love to you all, and thank you for your care and support, especially to those who have helped with this/ me with this already.

xxxx Eschani

The immediate responses were wonderful and very uplifting. Friends who were far away still offered the help that they could. I felt much love from them all, and it brightened my soul considerably. I received many emails, many texts, and many "energetic" hugs. Instantly, I didn't feel so alone.

Within forty-eight hours, I had someone offering to come for a ten-day holiday, which just happened to span before and after my four days away. She and Geoffrey were like sister and brother, so I knew it would work fine. I told Geoffrey that those were the dates she was coming to visit because that's what worked for her, and that he'd just have to be nice to her while I was away. What a relief! I was still going to be able to go to the competition. I felt as though I had won a battle. Yay for me.

One thing I found incredibly difficult was lying to Geoffrey. For his own peace of mind, because he thought that there was nothing wrong with him, I was lying to him for the first time ever. Along with the feeling of victory was a deep sadness underneath that this was the new reality of our relationship.

I needed help. I wasn't coping emotionally with this at all. To say I was hitting depression would be an understatement, but I was so overwhelmed with everything I just kept going around in circles. Even though I had an excellent understanding of many self-help tools, I was too far into crisis to be able to utilise all of these very well at that time.

My youngest daughter lived on the Sunshine Coast, only two hours north of us, with her husband and two young children. When I talked with her about Geoffrey's condition, she suggested looking up an organisation called Carers Queensland. She was studying for her certificate III in aged care, so I figured her information was up to date. I followed through with calling them as soon as I could.

I had to wait until Geoffrey was well and truly occupied at the other end of the house so I had some privacy. That took a while because we were inundated with different doctor's appointments, a new cardiologist, and more tests galore. I just felt so overwhelmed. There were so many things to do first.

Then Geoffrey told me that he thought he had a bit of a pain behind or in his ear—he couldn't tell me exactly where. Once I looked closely at his ear and neck, it was apparent that there was a swelling just under his ear. *Oh great, something else*, I thought. As it turned out, he had a bad ear infection. It took three courses of antibiotics and ear drops for it to clear up.

Once the ear infection was gone, some of the dementia symptoms disappeared too, and he was more "normal". That's when my severe case of denial began: *There's nothing really wrong with him, just some cognitive dysfunction due to his last surgery*. I thought that he'd be fine.

As it turned out, of course, he was somewhat better but nowhere near fine. The doctor, a geriatrician, was able to re-evaluate him, and the prognosis was extended to probably five to eight years rather than one or two, as previously suggested. I might not have to manage him on my own. I could breathe again. Things weren't perfect, but at least the train had slowed a little.

Insight – Two

Just because I knew that I could control my feelings didn't always mean I was able to do so 100 per cent of the time. I would ask myself, "What benefit am I getting out of feeling sad?" The answer was, "No benefit at all." So I'd take a big breath and breathe out *sad*, breathe out *overwhelmed*, breathe in *relaxed* and *calm*. I'd repeat this process, and I'd feel a little better.

I was unable to change the situation, so the only option was to find a way to deal with it. Otherwise, I would fall apart completely—which was *not* an option for me at all.

So I continued my self-empowerment processes. It didn't stop the feelings. What it did, though, was give me a way to deal with them without my feelings taking full control of me every minute and rendering me totally useless.

Asking yourself questions and being real with yourself with the answers is a very powerful self-empowerment tool. First, identify the feeling which keeps coming back to you and what you are making it mean about yourself. For example, you might feel out of control or overwhelmed. You could make this mean that you are not good enough to deal with the world, or because you are unable to sort things by yourself, that you as a person are lesser in some way. There may be many scenarios which will evoke this overwhelmed feeling. In reality, if you look back at your life, you will have felt overwhelmed millions of times. Ask yourself, *Have I felt overwhelmed well? Really well? Do I truly know this feeling of being overwhelmed to the core of me?*

Have you done this feeling of being overwhelmed well enough? What if, in essence, you have done this feeling well enough to have earned a degree in it? Having worked with and mentored a great many people, I can assure you the answer will usually be a resounding *yes*.

Once you realise that you have earned a degree in feeling overwhelmed, you can give yourself an internal certificate of achievement or an honours degree in feeling that old uncomfortable feeling. Now you can choose how you might prefer to feel instead. In your daily life, when the old automatic feeling comes up, you can remind yourself that you already have well and truly achieved that feeling. It is an old reality, past its use-by date.

Ask yourself, *Do I need to do it anymore?* No. Have a laugh at yourself for continuing to work on something that you have already achieved honours in. Now you can choose to respond to the world differently, take a breath, and move on.

The other good question to ask is, *What benefit am I getting out of feeling this way?* If you are honest, there might be (negative) pay-offs for feeling bad. For one, you get other people's sympathy, or what is called *negative nurturing*. You get to feel validated in feeling bad.

Is that a real benefit to you? No! You may be able to find something that you think is a benefit, but it will not be supporting you to be your powerful, positive self. This means that if you are being deeply honest and real with yourself, there will never be a true benefit in holding on to an old negative or bad feeling.

In this example, I used the feeling of being overwhelmed. Any negative feeling can be substituted here. The same questions apply. The ultimate goal is to move from the negative feeling to something positive, like peace, happiness, balance, or calm.

—•◆•—

There were days when Geoffrey was fairly normal, and my denial kicked in again. Then, within a day or two, I'd find my kitchen utensils in with the pots and pans, or my knife-block knives in one of the drawers or with the cups. Reality would hit anew—sadness, disbelief, frustration, anger, disappointment, and more.

A number of bad days followed, days where he was short-tempered and frustrated. He kept losing things. Where were his glasses? Had I seen them? Where did I put his medicine glass? I never moved his possessions, so I'd no idea what he had done with these things. Clearly anxious and annoyed, of course he got cross with me.

I was as patient as I could be each time as I gently calmed him down and told him not to worry and that we'd find them. "Oh look—is that your glasses over there?" I'd ask. It went on and on like this.

He snapped at me many times. If I asked him to pass me something, for example, I'd wait and wait and wait and breathe and then I'd ask him again. He'd get cross and grumble that I was *so* impatient or that I was hard to live with these days. My mind immediately went to that saying about the pot calling the kettle black. But I said nothing, and emotionally, it was really hard. I had never had to tippy-toe around him before. I felt it so deeply that I just needed to talk to a *real* person—a *normal* person.

I called the Dementia Help Line. Through my tears of frustration, I began to truly understand a little of what I was in for. I found that the person on the other end of the phone was immensely helpful and reinforced about being patient, about not having expectations, about not correcting him, about not trying to be logical, and about just letting things go. There were suggestions of some better language I could use so that Geoffrey didn't feel corrected, or feel wrong, or become so frustrated with me.

The helpline people offered information about the general pattern of dementia and what to expect in terms of deterioration. One thing discussed was his inability to plan or make decisions. I knew this one already! It was the simplest of things sometimes that confused him. We'd be at a cafe. I'd go to order the coffee. I'd ask him to pick a table anywhere, inside or out, wherever he liked. After I'd ordered and paid, I would turn around and see that he was standing a few feet away from me. He'd been unable to decide where to sit. I had to make that decision.

Gradually, over a period of months, I learned not to ask him to choose or to make very many decisions if at all possible. If I asked him why he hadn't sat anywhere, for example, he'd just grumpily reply, "How am I supposed to know where you want to sit?"

One of the silly things that bothered me at this time was his fanciful stories. For example, he'd see an L-plate on the car belonging to a neighbour and confidently say, "She's a driving instructor." When I enquired further, I found that it's what he had decided the woman of that house did for a living. The fact that there was a teenager in the household and the L-plate was only on the car occasionally, plus there weren't any driving instructor school markings/advertising on the car, had no relevance to him. He saw, he thought, he decided, and that was that. No use arguing, because he would only get upset or angry. It was only *my* logic which needed to be heard, and that was just not going to happen.

So many little things he was no longer logical about took me by surprise to begin with, because he had always been a fairly logical person. In the beginning, I'd ask him what he was talking about or how he'd come to that conclusion, but his explanations always frustrated me. Once I felt frustrated, I was not able to stop myself from snapping at him.

I'd try to make him see common sense or his lack of logic. Bad idea! He'd get very grumpy with me or turn it around and say that I was a know-it-all. Sometimes I'd say that his conclusions were ridiculous and he'd get very cross and things went nowhere. I just became more annoyed and felt isolated. Once I realised this, I'd do my best to reply, "Oh, do you think so?" or "Oh, right," or something similar.

What I am explaining here is that I had to choose what I was going to make matter. In the grand scheme of things, did it matter if I had to make all the decisions? I was capable, so I could choose to make that not matter. Did I need to make it matter if he came up with unlikely stories about other people, places, or things? No, I didn't need to. However, saying that and actually letting it go so that I didn't make it matter took a lot of effort sometimes. I knew this was the best way to deal with these things, but we had communicated so differently in the past. I was struggling to change my habits and my expectations.

Many of my interactions with Geoffrey were automatic, as we had been together for so long and I had become very used to being able to communicate with him well. Now I had to continually decide what to make matter. I reminded myself that if I didn't make these things matter, they would cease to bother me. My feelings were mine alone.

I also realised that when Geoffrey told his stories to other people, I felt uncomfortable or embarrassed for him. When I felt that way, I also felt obligated to explain, either about the story to put it right or about Geoffrey's condition. This was actually taking responsibility for others—both Geoffrey and his audience. In fact, I only needed to take emotional responsibility for myself. I didn't need to make incorrect stories matter, because Geoffrey was how he was and how people took him was their business. If it was important, and they were confused by what Geoffrey told them, they'd come to me at some stage, and I'd put them right about whatever it was.

3

Often, difficulties arose when we were going somewhere. For example, Geoffrey had an appointment to get his hearing aids checked and have a hearing test. This would entail a standard hearing test, and then the audiologist would digitally reset his hearing aids to the best setting for Geoffrey's current hearing levels.

Off we went. After I had driven about ten minutes down the road, Geoffrey said, "I don't have my hearing aids with me. I might need them, mightn't I?"

Oh my God, yes, you need your hearing aids! It was another two hundred metres before I could turn around. We got home, and after I quizzed him as to where his hearing aids might be, I dashed inside, got them, and attempted to drive calmly down the road to his appointment. Fortunately, I had a hands-free phone in the car, and I phoned ahead to let them know we'd be ten minutes late. I hated being late, but I had to make it not matter. *Just go with the flow, one big breath and then another!*

I had been told to expect toilet problems: to expect him to forget to flush to begin with, possibly followed by needing to be taken to the toilet. So far, we hadn't had toileting problems, but sometimes I found he had missed or perhaps had multiple streams, and he was totally unaware that he had flooded the floor.

Once again, an incident occurred as we were about to go out: We were headed to the dentist. Geoffrey had broken a tooth. I just popped in to use the toilet before we left, only to find a very wet floor. *Oh great,* I thought. I couldn't just leave it; it was a hot day, so the toilet would stink by the time we got home. I cleaned it up quickly with the intention to mop the floor properly when we returned.

As I jumped into the car to head off, Geoffrey gruffly questioned me about how long I had taken, because he didn't want to be late. I wasn't thinking about his dementia and told him that I was cleaning up the toilet floor that he'd left a mess on. Bad response! I knew immediately I'd said the wrong thing.

He acted like a child defending himself. He pouted and said he didn't know he'd done it. I told him that I knew he didn't do it deliberately, but it had to be cleaned up. Obviously, he felt bad and felt criticised, because what followed was a diatribe about how I was always finding fault with him and how he was always doing the wrong thing and he couldn't do anything right.

I took a deep breath, because by this time I was driving, and inside, I just felt so angry, so overwhelmed, and so frustrated. I knew it was an extreme overreaction, but in that split millisecond, I truly wanted to slam my foot onto the accelerator and smash us into a tree. It would have been so easy! Instead, I braked. I breathed deeply and continued driving normally. If he was acting like a child, I had to treat him like a child.

In a stern voice, I told him to pull himself together and stop acting like a hard-done-by little boy. I reminded him that he'd asked what took so long, and I'd told him. End of story! I wasn't complaining, just answering what he'd asked.

Suddenly, the real Geoffrey returned, and he calmly said, "Thank you." That was that for him. He was happy again. As I drove to the dentist, though, it took a while for me to calm down, because all I really wanted to do was stop the car and have a cry.

From a personal growth/self-development or spiritual perspective, I knew that everything we experience could teach us something. Boy oh boy, I clearly had to learn greater patience! But beyond feeling impatient, truly what I was feeling was powerlessness. At that time, I felt as though there was no way out, and I was totally powerless to change anything.

INSIGHT – THREE

When we feel powerless, we believe there is no other way to fix the problem, and it is normal to become angry. Anger is a powerful feeling, and we automatically go for it because it gives a powerful feeling—albeit a false sense of power. It does not solve the problem at all.

Why do we feel powerless? In my experiences with Geoffrey, my powerless feeling was a result of judgements on and expectations of how things should be or how I thought they were. I was lulled into a false sense of security in that Geoffrey's behaviour was fairly normal most of the time. It created within me an expectation that he would respond in a normal manner to things. So when he did not respond normally, I reacted with anger and frustration because my expectations were not being met. This was a good lesson for me to let go of my judgements and expectations. Inside me, I knew that he was unable to change what was happening in his brain. I had to just allow what was happening to be OK.

When we let go of expectations, we create an easier life for ourselves. It also allows us to view things from another side of the brick—to view the situation from a new perspective. Releasing the expectations of normal and allowing what is to just be how it is, without judging it as not OK, makes dealing with the situation at hand much easier. I needed to stay with the reality of how Geoffrey was rather than how I expected him to be. I did find that breathing out my anger and frustration helped. It gave me a space to let go of the expectation of receiving a normal response from him.

Anger and frustration are reactions to expectations not being met and often a result of past experiences where we felt hurt in some way. Reactions are not helpful to the situation; however, a response will be. Responses come from the adult part of ourselves where we are aware of the actuality of the situation. There are no judgements, no expectations, no blame. Responding is powerful and opens up the ability to see other perspectives.

When I eventually had a chance to contact Carers Queensland, I made an appointment to go see someone to find out what services were offered and what help might be available to me. The gentleman I saw was helpful, understanding, and patient. To some degree, I felt that this could be a good lifeline for me.

I discovered that they did have some support groups, but most of them met only monthly and were a fair distance away. Once I saw their calendar of events, I found that in that particular month, the couple of groups that might be relevant to me were being held on days when I already had events booked—chorus concert, visiting relatives, doctor/specialist visits, my working week in Melbourne, and so on.

It was a couple of months before I was able to attend anything. I chose a craft morning with Carers Queensland as an easy start. I love doing craft things, and I enjoyed it from that perspective. However, it was of no use at all with regards to any discussion or support around caring for someone with dementia.

Eventually, I did attend a social morning, followed by an excellent full-day workshop. I learned a great deal about how to best communicate with Geoffrey, and I began to understand the social implications and how my life had and would continue to change. In short, I had to take charge of absolutely everything and do it in a way in which *he* felt heard, empowered and comfortable. Oh, what fun! *I will do my best,* I thought. I also knew that I would have to be very kind and patient with myself first.

We made it through Christmas (2016) and the New Year. We had family stay with us for two weeks, and in that time, I really noticed Geoffrey's withdrawal. He wasn't coping with the noise and activity of the children. Geoffrey had never been a life-of-the-party type of person, but he would usually contribute to conversations here and there. I did notice that he was away in his own world a little more, and he participated less.

The weather was hot, and everyone enjoyed using the swimming pool every day, often multiple times a day. Geoffrey, however, went into the pool only once during those two weeks. Most days, he disappeared into the bedroom and had a nap. He was unable to help in the kitchen at all because his routine had been changed. There were more people to feed, more cups or glasses, more plates, more cutlery, more food being prepared or served, and so on.

I struggled to not feel abandoned by Geoffrey. My daughters and my son-in-law seemed to be helping so much and pitching in with everything, which is how it needed to be when there were so many people to cater for. The busyness, though, created a barrier for Geoffrey to participate normally. The household routine was different, and he found it hard to cope with. And so he withdrew, talked very little, and hardly interacted with anyone.

Even the grandchildren had to work hard to get their pa's attention or to get a response out of him when they proudly showed him something they'd made, created, or done. I loved having the family around and spending time with my adorable grandchildren, but I found it very difficult to meet Geoffrey's needs as well. It's hard to explain; it felt wonderful to have them around but awful too, as I could see Geoffrey becoming more and more withdrawn.

It took a week or so for Geoffrey to return to normal—and I use that term very loosely! Maybe it would be more correct to say that things returned to a more regular pattern. I found it extremely difficult to cope with being on my own again with him. I simply felt sad all the time—hurt and sad. The feeling of being abandoned by him persisted.

INSIGHT - FOUR

Everything in your world is a reflection of yourself. Feeling abandoned by someone is a red flag, you could say, to the fact that I was also abandoning myself. I realised that I was not allowing myself to have enough support. I was trying to mostly to do this thing on my own. We are connected spiritual beings. When we allow ourselves to connect at a spiritual or energy level to a greater power or energy, then we generate connection to something greater than ourselves.

Connecting on a spiritual or energy level will mean different things for each of us. For some, this means help from God. For others, it means full meditation or prayer, or maybe it is quiet breathing and gathering energy into our centre until we feel settled. When we allow that moment of connection, many more things will flow in our lives. Often what will then flow into our lives will be some sort of support.

I clearly needed some support. It was time I allowed it.

4

It was time to get some real help. I needed some time off. Geoffrey was with it enough to know what was going on most of the time, so I could not suggest that he go somewhere for respite, but I did need time to go have a coffee with a friend or just get away from him for short periods.

I looked to register on the My Aged Care website (the Australian government website for older Australians), The site itself was confusing, so I phoned. In order for me to speak for and on behalf of Geoffrey, he had to give his consent. Not a problem; I told him it was to register to get some home help for me. I put the phone on speaker. He gave the OK and gave his full name and date of birth … well, not quite. He got the year incorrect.

I corrected him, and he looked at me quizzically and asked, "Are you sure"? He looked like a lost child in that moment. Then he gave our home address. The house number he gave was also incorrect; he had no idea of the postcode or the phone number.

He was clearly embarrassed, saying that if we'd given him time, he would've been able to bring it all to mind. I knew that was not the case, but I reassured him that it did not matter. Then I removed myself to another room to finish the conversation and organise some home respite. I just had to wait however long it was going to be—days or weeks—to receive a phone call from whichever agency would be supplying the service. I sincerely hoped that it didn't cost the earth.

Meanwhile, we just kept plodding along, having good days and bad. On one occasion, after I had been on the phone to Tamara and we'd been discussing some work stuff, Geoffrey enquired about what we'd been talking about. I told him. I didn't think anything of it. There was nothing unusual in his request. He had, in the past, liked to be kept informed about work information, even if he'd had less to do with the everyday running of things.

On this occasion, however, Tamara and I had been talking about emails that had to be sent about a person who was returning to mastery class in time for the next session in Melbourne in six weeks. We had been having a quiet, easy morning, and I was shocked at Geoffrey's sudden annoyance. He became very upset with me, as he said he had not been told about this at all.

When I reminded him of the letter that had arrived recently from this person asking about returning to the class, Geoffrey denied even knowing anything about it. Oh, he knew there had been a letter, but, "How am I supposed to know who it was from? You didn't tell me."

No matter what I said, he got more and more cross, and he swore that he didn't know anything about it. Of course I had told him, and of course we had talked about this person returning to the class, and of course he'd had input, but in his mind, he was adamant that he knew nothing about it.

Then along comes the accusations: "You and Tamara talk about everything." And "I'm not included in your conversations." And so it went on. I might add here that often, when I was on the phone to Tamara, I would put the phone onto speaker mode so that he could be included. Often, though, he'd walk away and go and do his crossword puzzle, so I would continue to talk with Tam in another room.

On a logical level, I understood it all. He could not mentally keep up with conversations, so he would remove himself. I knew that I did keep him informed, but he didn't remember. Emotionally, though, I felt hurt when he crossly and accusingly said these things and adamantly accused me of deliberately keeping him in the dark and not telling him things. He claimed I did not tell him and that I just thought I'd told him. His tone of voice was awful as he angrily swore that I didn't tell him stuff.

This was not my darling! I didn't know this person! This was another Geoffrey—a mean and accusing, angry, rude man. He was hateful when he was like this. He was hard to love, but I did love him. It was just really, really hard. I was so sad as I wrote this, my tears fully flowed.

When I returned to the room Geoffrey was in, he was fine, just like nothing had happened. I was struggling to look and sound normal; I was still upset. I had no idea how to be normal, but I had to make lunch and be normal.

———◆———

The weeks progressed. I reached out to Carers Queensland, and they put me on to Community Care Services. Early February, the regional assessment service person, Jacqui, came to see us in order to organise some services. I was *so* grateful. She arranged for a podiatrist to come and look after Geoffrey's feet every six weeks. She organised a physiotherapist to come and assess him with a view to them coming and working with Geoffrey regularly to help reduce his risk of falls. (He had fallen over, or rather tripped, three times in recent months.) Lastly, she put into place some home help: two hours once a fortnight.

Jacqui was helpful, friendly, and very understanding. I felt as if there was some hope for my sanity. Oh, my goodness! What an enormous help these ideas were. I was unable to express just how much I thought these things would assist me. I knew I needed more support, but this was a fantastic start. The fact that we only had to pay a contribution towards these services made it possible, too.

Jacqui also recommended an aged care assessment team (ACAT) assessment for Geoffrey so that he could receive funding for greater services at home plus possible future care—either respite care or full-time care. The assessment is required for a person who needs to be approved for government-funded services, including a nursing home (aged care home), home care, residential aged care, transition care, or respite.

Everything took a few weeks to organise. Once we had the podiatrist, the physio, and the fortnightly home help in place, I felt considerably less stressed. I was also getting used to letting things go more easily. I took lots more deep breaths, and I phoned friends sometimes just so I could chat with normal people.

I was still so used to Geoffrey being his old self that it was sometimes easy to forget his condition. Then he would try to help me with something, usually ending in some sort of disaster because he was no longer able to manage whatever tool was required properly or safely. He was no longer able to make sensible or safe decisions. I'd get annoyed with him when he'd break something or just stand there with no idea how to carry out whatever simple task I gave him. He'd get upset because he was only trying to help me.

This was a tough one! Geoffrey had been a kind and gentle man, always wishing to assist me whenever he could. So that was still his motivation, his duty. Now that he was not capable of doing this very often, I did my best to let him know that he didn't need to do it anymore; it was my turn to look after him. He just had to accept that there were things he couldn't do anymore and that I thought no less of him because of it.

The tables had turned, and it was my turn to help him. To some degree, I know he understood this, even though it was a hard habit for him to break. He kept trying to help, but he did begin to respond better when I said that I could do this or that myself.

Now, home maintenance has never been my forte, but I was learning new skills, and I found that I was able to use many tools I'd never tried before. If I found that it was beyond me, I waited until someone was there who could assist, and I asked. I think that's called "allowing support"—not something that I had been very good at in the past. It was definitely something I was going to have to do more of in the future.

In March 2017, we had one of our weeks in Melbourne. During that week, Geoffrey developed shingles (herpes zoster) and was in considerable pain. Tamara and I managed to get him to a doctor, and he was prescribed some antiviral medication, which we got into him pretty quick. He was in considerable discomfort, and painkillers were the only way he could get relief. I worked, and he rested that week. My daughter Tamara was a mighty power of support that week, and I got through it OK. Thank you, Tamara. I love you.

Once we were home again, I made sure that Geoffrey had plenty of rest and got all his medication into him, and he recovered within a few weeks. But it was as if I could no longer deny the reality.

Geoffrey had dementia—now I got it. Many others didn't. It was interesting to see others (friends) attempting to do what I had done: treat Geoffrey as normal and expect normal responses from him. It just wasn't going to happen. I found myself needing to educate others and teach them not to ask him remembering questions or how-to questions, and also not to ask him "where is" questions. To do so only plunged him into confusion and gave him a sense of inadequacy. When this happened, he would shut down and not communicate at all. He had always been a quiet man. It was subtle; often others would not notice, but I did.

We had houseguests for a couple of weeks. It rained. It rained a lot. The weather system came from the end of Cyclone Debbie, and we had huge downpours. The rain prevented our friends from going out and about as much as they might have liked. Many areas around us were flooded. Geoffrey seemed OK on the outside, but he was struggling having people there and having our routine changed a little.

My daughter and son-in-law from the Sunshine Coast stayed a couple of weekends and began to paint the exterior of our house for us. That was fantastic, as it needed to be done and was going to cost us a small fortune if we got a painter in to do it. The idea was that they'd come down every few weeks and just keep at it until the job was done. All I had to do was look after the kids and most of the meals.

I had to work fairly hard keeping the littlies away from Geoffrey, and in order to keep the extra noise and movement away from him, I took the kids outside. They "helped" me with the garden. We pruned a great deal, the children with their scissors, me with the hedge-trimmer. I checked in on Geoffrey regularly so see that he was OK.

When the activities (inside or out) were too much for Geoffrey, I suggested that he move to another room and read or watch TV by himself or nap. He managed OK so long as I managed him well. I made sure that he rested while I walked the children and the dogs to the park one morning. Whilst appreciating the great job being done with the painting, Geoffrey was still happy when they left, as all the activity around him had tired him. I made a mental note: I would just have to keep managing him well each weekend they came.

--------◆•◆•◆--------

In April 2017, Geoffrey was assessed by Christie, a member of the ACAT team. Christie was very experienced, and she handled Geoffrey very well. She explained that some of her questions might seem nosy, but that was her job—she had to ask lots of personal questions in order to get the best support services for him. Fortunately, Geoffrey was having a very good morning, and he took it all in well and was even alert enough to make a joke with her during the process.

Some of her questions he was able to answer, but many he couldn't, or he answered with the wrong information. But because he was good that morning, he was OK with me correcting the information or adding to it for Christie. With some questions, he just turned to me with a questioning look, and I gave Christie the information she needed.

On a difficult day, he would have become grumpy and uncooperative. I would not have been able to answer or say any of that with him present, and I would have needed a lot of time with Christie on my own. Geoffrey even told her that he was having a good day. Overall, the process went smoothly, and he was approved for government funding for services at home or in a care home if/when the time came. A level-3 package was approved, which meant that the government would supply funding for Geoffrey to have a level of care at home, thus keeping him out of residential care for as long as possible.

It was now just over a year since his diagnosis. I found that I really needed to have time away from Geoffrey. This was a foreign feeling for me, because we'd been together so long, worked side by side, and spent 24/7 together in the past, and it had worked extremely well. Now it was different; my patience was running thin, and I felt stressed. Christie had seen that my stress levels were right up there, and she offered to get someone from Alzheimer's Australia (now called Dementia Australia) in touch with me with a view to getting Geoffrey out of the house for a day a week to give me a break. I said, "Yes please!" Geoffrey looked suspicious and said, "What for?"

Before the lovely Leanne from the local Alzheimer's Australia centre came, I chatted to Geoffrey about how I'd really love to do an art class, but it would mean I was out once a week for hours and I would worry about him being on his own. Of course, he told me that he'd be OK. However, over the next few weeks, there were times that he struggled with some things, and I reminded him that these were what I'd worry about if I was out for several hours.

By the time Leanne came, he'd had time to think about it, and he agreed to go on a minibus trip once a week, but "only if the people are not too far gone! They need to be OK to talk to." Leanne made sure that he got the message that he'd be with people who only just occasionally forgot things, just like he did.

I breathed a sigh of relief. I booked in to art class with a beautiful teacher only twenty minutes away. Hooray! I was going to be free for a day, one day a week. I hadn't done any art for over seventeen years, so I was looking forward to that creative and meditative space/time again.

5

hile we waited for the government home care package funding to be approved and then for it to come through, we kept on with the services which had been put into place: two hours of cleaning once a fortnight and a podiatrist every six weeks. Geoffrey had tried using the physiotherapist who would come twice a week, but he had become bored with it, so instead, I was taking him to the hydrotherapy pool once a week. My friend Lyn, who had rheumatoid arthritis, was also keen to do hydrotherapy, so the three of us went each week, and it was enjoyable for all.

The weekly Thursday bus trips were working OK, but Geoffrey was not thrilled with them. I made a pact with him that he could change over to something else once the funding came through and we could work with a different service provider.

By July 2017, we finally had some funding, albeit not as much as he had been approved for. He was on the priority list for the full funding, but at least with some funding, we could get started. We signed up with Blue Care, and we would have a care worker come to our home four hours a week. Because the full funding had not yet been granted, the Thursday bus trip with the Alzheimer Australia group would continue. Geoffrey was not altogether pleased about this, as he was not really enjoying the bus trips. I felt a bit mean making him go, but I really needed my time off. His condition was slowly getting worse, but very slowly.

One morning, I discovered one of my lovely new plants which my youngest daughter had planted in the side garden had been pulled out and broken. The root ball looked OK, and I went in search of a tool to dig the garden and replant it. Geoffrey saw me and said he thought it was a weed, and he'd pulled it out.

Many unkind thoughts jumped into my head, as well as, *that's not logical, as my daughter had planted some exactly the same in the front garden, and they looked beautiful and were flowering.* But dementia kills logic! My plant, a delightful red plant, dark red foliage and lovely white puff ball flowers, might survive. I coolly informed him that it was *not* a weed, but I was taking lots of deep breaths. Then I just laughed. My goodness, this is crazy! He thought he was helping!

Another morning, Geoffrey decided he needed to do some stretches. Good idea—he needed to keep those muscles working. But he was not being logical, again. He was using the step in the bathroom, up to the bath. The step is a big one, and he lost his balance and reeled backwards, colliding with the wall. When I suggested that he could do his stretches in a safer location, he became very angry with me. Because logic didn't work, anything I said or suggested only made him more cross.

I was getting frustrated, because I could see how unstable he was, and I feared him falling heavily and doing himself some damage. He strongly proclaimed that he was OK and that he knew what he was doing, and I should just leave him alone.

Of course, I became angry, and my inner teenage-self became furious. *I'll bloody well leave you alone*, I thought. *I'll just leave you here, and I'll pick up Lyn and take her to hydrotherapy and leave you here on your own!* My feelings were flying everywhere. I felt helpless and powerless, unappreciated, hurt, and sad. This concoction of feelings led to an enormous amount of anger within me, so I removed myself immediately from Geoffrey's presence. Getting angry with him was not going to lead to anything good.

I went for a walk. I left him alone for a short while at home while I walked off my anger, sadness, and helplessness. When I returned, I discovered that he hadn't even noticed that I'd been out. How bizarre! I just had to see the funny side of things, or I would truly go mad. Then I laughed and cried at the same time. I breathed deeply a great deal until I felt better.

INSIGHT – FIVE

When we, as young children, are denied what we want, or when we feel criticized, misunderstood, or not empathised with, we experience hurt. In feeling this hurt, we burst into tears. Sometimes we retreat in misery or become angry. Underneath this reaction of anger remains the feeling of hurt and the powerlessness to change things. In this state, we are unable to be rational, just like children. Neither are we able to be rational when we act like this as grown-ups. This is just being, and playing out as, our hurt child-self.

When we grow up and our buttons are pushed or we feel threatened, the great majority of people revert to childhood reactive behaviours. We blame others and sometimes want to hurt someone in retaliation for our own inner hurt. This aspect of us which immediately wants to argue back, make someone pay, or generally get back at someone is our teenage-self doing what a teen would do in reacting with what feels powerful: anger and vengeance. This reaction is played out in order to cover up hurt feelings.

Of course, this is counterproductive and will always return negative results because blaming or shaming only gives us the illusion of being back in control. It doesn't resolve any conflict. It only escalates it.

Once we recognise these behaviours as our child-self or our teen-self, we are in a position to choose adult behaviours. Adult behaviours allow us to choose our responses instead of our old automatic reactions. There are many processes to assist us in doing this. Healing our inner hurt child takes some time and requires us to have a great deal of love and patience with ourselves. If you are interested in knowing more, you could begin by listening to the "Inner Child Healing" audio available at http://www.tikashi.com.au/product/inner-child-healing/

On the way to art class that week, I expressed my frustrations to my friend Lyn, and I told her about my angry thoughts and how close she came to being taken to hydrotherapy on her own.

"Ooh!" she exclaimed. "Your inner teenager really came out."

She was spot on, and I knew it. I didn't need a shoulder to cry on. I didn't need to be pitied. I just needed to vent and be understood. It was perfect. It was a great acknowledgement for me, and we laughed about it. Ah it's so good to have someone who really understands me. Thank you, Lyn. I love you.

❦

By September 2017, we'd settled into more of a regular routine, and I was reacting far less and remembering to be gentle and light, laugh or joke, placate, gently guide him, and in general take the blame as often as needed in order to keep him calm. He'd get bursts of frustration, and I was the target. I was learning to just cop it, not to argue back or say anything that he might hear as criticism. It was not my natural way of being, so I didn't always succeed, but I was doing better. Logic would get us nowhere. Dementia had well and truly killed logic.

I'd learned not to tell him that we'd seen a TV episode of something many times before, because he'd just blame me for making things up or for thinking I'd seen everything! Instead, I sat with him in front of the TV and played my phone games or checked out Facebook while re-watching programs we've seen many times before.

In between all these things, we had good times, of course. There were times when Geoffrey was not demanding. In fact, he reverted back to his caring and considerate self. As his heart was not really strong, often he'd offer to help me with things that I knew he would not be able to do easily, so mostly I told him that I was OK and that I could do it. It was still good to see him smile and to be able to make him laugh occasionally.

In years past, Geoffrey would edit soundtracks from our/my work sessions with people. He'd use a program on the computer, and we'd give people copies of their sessions in which the sound had been cleaned up, long pauses removed, and so forth. Geoffrey thought that he was still doing that, as I was still giving him soundtracks to edit. In reality, I was the one who did the editing by this time, because the quality of Geoffrey's work? Well, let's just say that if people received the raw recording, they'd be *far* better off! This was one way in which I could keep his self-esteem up. He felt that he was doing something useful and he was helping me.

After the last trip to Melbourne, Geoffrey said that he wanted me to give him some recordings to edit. I copied some of the sessions onto his hard drive. Up until now, he had known what to do in order to open files in the editing software on his computer. This time, he angrily complained to me that the files weren't working, because all he could get was the sound of them. He wanted a printout.

This initially had me stumped. The work was usually done on the computer; there was nothing to print. I gently questioned him to find out what the problem was, and of course, he became short with me. I was clearly an idiot. What was the matter with me? I used to understand things. Why wasn't I listening to him? I was able to laugh and say that yes, I was clearly at fault, because I couldn't understand.

Then I asked him to show me. I saw that he was double-clicking the file, and the automatic audio player on the computer was playing the sound. Aha! That was the sound he was referring to. Once I opened up the sound editing software and then opened a file for him where he could *see* the sound on the screen, I realised that this was the printout he was referring to. He'd just totally forgotten that he had to use a program, the sound-editing program, in order to edit the file.

Once Geoffrey saw the program open on the screen and could see his "printout" of the sound, he immediately went into a volley of reasons why he had forgotten. He was clearly uncomfortable every time he realised that he had forgotten something. This meant that every time he realised, he grumpily came up with excuses, reasons, and justifications. When that occurred, I attempted to calm him and kept reassuring him that it did not matter, we'd sorted it now, relax, it's OK. Then he settled down. We moved on.

There were many more examples of him forgetting things, and the list was growing longer every month. We were due to return to Melbourne in March 2018. At this stage, with that being six months away, I wasn't sure if he would be up to it.

———◆•◆•◆———

Every day presented challenges for Geoffrey. Filling the car with petrol, for example—I'd usually go inside and pay while Geoffrey filled the tank, but I noticed one day that he was having trouble working out how to rehang the pump nozzle. If his razor needed recharging, sometimes he was fine with it, and other times he'd have trouble working out how to plug it in. It took him longer to unlock the letterbox to get our mail. I had long ago placed a red dot and a green dot on the microwave to indicate the off and on buttons, but he was taking longer to work it out. It was all about the little things—the everyday little things.

People saw him when they visited and proclaimed how good he was. And yes, sitting at the table chatting, he was mostly fine, because he would only contribute when he could follow the conversation. At those times, he sounded OK. He looked OK. Everything appeared fine. Once they'd gone home, the problems would start.

After one visit, Geoffrey said that he would fill the dishwasher and turn it on. Good idea; the dishwasher was almost full anyway. I went out to hang the washing and came back to find that the dishwasher was not on. Upon closer inspection, I saw that he had put the dishwasher tablet into its compartment, and although the machine was turned on, the start button had not been pressed.

That was no big deal, you might think. The problem arose when he saw me looking at it and opening it. Then he growled to me that he'd put it on and I should just leave it be. Before I could quietly just press the start button, he was telling me that he *did* put it on, that he wasn't stupid, and that I didn't need to check it.

Once he actually saw that the machine had not even begun to wash, he started a diatribe about how these machines just don't work even though he pressed all the buttons. He was very agitated, and it took a bit of work to calm him down and reassure him that it did not matter, we'd got it going now, and so on. It was all about the little things. It took a mountain of energy to remain calm, and often I just had to allow him to blame me for stuff, because to argue went nowhere. He had no logic.

6

I believe and fully know that we all have control over our reactions, responses, and feelings—although not, of course, once dementia sets in. Yet I have struggled to feel in command of my feelings, my thoughts, and my reactions or responses since Geoffrey's dementia has progressed. This doesn't mean that I'm not allowed to feel sad or frustrated. It means that I, and only I, have a choice as to how I feel and how my life is. Internally, I can choose to be constantly annoyed and feel blamed and/or hard done by, or I can choose to let things move past me.

Many people might argue that we have no control over how we feel and that the words and actions of others affect us. When we live in that perspective, we are at the mercy of the world; we are at the mercy of the words and actions of others. What I am saying is that it doesn't need to be this way. In essence, the more we mould ourselves or change ourselves in order to be liked, to be approved of, or to not be hurt, the less we can truly be ourselves.

You are the only one living your life, and I am the only one living mine. Working with this means that I have total freedom with how I choose to be in any given moment. This is incredibly empowering, as nothing or no one can affect me unless I allow it to be so.

———◆———

I knew that I had control over my feelings and my reactions or responses. In theory, that worked well, and in my regular adult life, that had always worked well also. The tough bit came when what was going on mirrored events or feelings I had as a child.

Let me briefly explain. I came from an incredibly dysfunctional family. I'm the firstborn, and my only full sister was four years younger. My mother had very low self-esteem and was the eternal victim. My father was a cruel, a narcissist. He abused my mother emotionally and physically. She ended up in hospital on more than one occasion.

I was yelled at, called names, told that I was an idiot, blamed every time my sister cried, smacked across the face, and thrown across the room. I was beaten black and blue, shaken, kicked, and spat on. My father also seriously sexually abused me from around the age of 5 until I was almost 11. He made sure that I would not tell anyone by making me totally terrified of being in even greater trouble.

It was only because I was an extremely strong soul that I survived at all. Inside me, I knew that I was a better person than my father could ever be and that he could not break me or my spirit. As soon as I was able, I left school, got a job, and moved out of the toxic environment.

Without dismissing all that had occurred, over the years I came to see that all of my experiences had built who I was. I was strong, intelligent, wise, compassionate, and caring. I thoroughly loved having my own family and modelled it as much as I could to *not* be as my original family had been. My parenting style was very different from my parents'. I did still harbour some anger inside me as a young woman, and I know I yelled at my kids more than I might have otherwise done. Regardless, they have all turned out to be adults I am proud of, and we have good relationships with each other.

I have consciously worked on my belief systems as a result of my past conditioning, and for the most part, I have been able to function from an adult space, without anxiety or a great deal of worry. I predominantly listened to my heart more and made decisions based on balance and being peaceful inside, so I could enjoy each now moment in a loving way.

———————•◆•———————

Living in the now is a phrase that many people are familiar with these days. Actually, living this way in our society takes practice. The idea is really to not bring any old baggage from past events or experiences into whatever is going on in your life right now. It's about living from the heart every day, moment by moment, with only what is in front of us right now, not looking through a lens of the past. We must remember what is important, right now in every moment.

A quote that reminds me of this very eloquently is by Iain Thomas: "and every day the world will drag you by the hand, yelling, 'This is important! And this is important! You need to worry about this! And this!' And each day, it is up to you to yank your hand back, put it on your heart, and say, 'No. This is what's important.'"

Society puts so many demands upon us. Only we can decide what we are going to make the most important thing. When we live now, for now, without buying into a *have to* or *should* dictating our lives, we are able to give from the heart and receive likewise.

Each one of us makes those decisions many times every day. Usually we are so conditioned by the expectations of others, of society, and of our own upbringing and past experiences that we don't even notice we are making these decisions. That's why, for conscious and peaceful living, we need to slow down to bring our awareness into the now moment. From this space, we can make conscious decisions as to what is right in that moment. Breathe, listen, and take action from a place of peace.

———————•◆•———————

At the time with Geoffrey's dementia, I struggled once again with being blamed and with overwhelming sadness. I was finding it hard to come to terms with the difficulty of shrugging things off and feeling OK. *What is the matter with me?* I thought to myself. I had been teaching people to deal with difficulties in their lives for years and years. I was using the tools and techniques I'd taught others, but it just didn't seem to stick, and this created more frustration within me.

Of course, the "taking the blame" stuff triggered my childhood experiences, and I felt it was unfair. I figured that's normal. What was not normal for *me* was the trouble that I was having to be able to let it go, as it was only a childhood feeling and didn't belong to the now moment. I needed to work very, very hard each time in order to choose to feel good again and balanced. Sometimes I was successful, and sometimes I buried any bad feelings and just got on with things.

———◆———

As I was listening to and editing one of the mentoring sessions we'd had with a group recently in Melbourne, oh, how the pennies dropped! I really heard—I mean I *really* heard—the answer I needed. In the soundtrack, there was a conversation with Darryl (client, mastery mentor, and friend). He had been having some personal difficulties where he found it difficult to return to balance at times, even when he knew he was harbouring what we might call "negative" feelings. (I identified with this.) It was as if, because he *hadn't chosen* to feel bad, feeling bad was because of external circumstances. So how was he able *just choose* to feel good again?

Well, everything just pinged for me. I was doing the exact same thing. That is blame: blaming someone or something outside of myself for my own feelings. I was blaming Geoffrey for how he was, even though I knew he couldn't help it. Internally, I was making myself a victim all over again. I was feeling powerless to change my feelings, because I thought that I hadn't chosen to feel bad.

I knew that every one of us has a choice in every moment, and that's the truth. No matter what goes on in our lives, we can choose how we feel, even if we have been thrown into feeling bad by others' behaviour or words, by circumstances, by having old realities triggered, and by not consciously choosing to feel bad. We still have that choice, and it is as easy as remembering that and allowing a choice to be happy, to be OK. Phew, did I feel better? Yes! Thank you, Darryl. I love you.

It's the same way with sadness—but I was told that sadness is also part of grieving. I was grieving who I was losing, the parts of him which were gone already, and the future which would be missed. I allowed myself to grieve, and I also allowed myself to return to balance and happiness. Life was good.

Mostly, Geoffrey was happy and blissfully unaware that anything was wrong. He expressed how much he loved me on a regular basis. He was easy to please with many things. He loved whatever I cooked for him and in general was undemanding. This, in a way, was why it was more difficult when his memory went or he became anxious or grumpy. It just was not who he usually was—or should I say, who he had been.

For example, he would "spit the dummy" when he couldn't find what he wanted on the computer or the internet. He became angrier and angrier and blamed the computer. Of course, it was what he was or was not clicking that was the real problem. Inevitably, he'd call me to come *immediately* to fix the damn thing. He continually had troubles when he tried to use the iPad, and once again, it was the stupid thing's fault. Once again, I was expected to drop whatever I was doing at the time *immediately* and go to his aid.

At the end of September 2017, before a trip to the doctor to have his ears checked for wax (he'd been having trouble hearing more from the left ear and the audiologist didn't want to change his hearing aid settings before his ears were checked), I went to the picture framer. There was one portrait and two bird pictures which I'd drawn that needed to be framed. On the way, Geoffrey commented that he hadn't been there before.

He had in fact been with me the last time I'd gone to the same framer. I made the mistake of saying that he'd been with me about three months ago when I'd framed a portrait I'd done of my granddaughter. I took a breath; he'd been good that day, but he had absolutely no recollection whatsoever that he'd been there before. I just said OK when he insisted that, "You must've been with someone else, it wasn't me, because *I* have *never* been there before!"

It now appeared that chunks of memory had gone, yet other memories were very clear. He was unable to recall a Japanese restaurant and a particular dish which we used to really love having when we were in Melbourne. He could remember some shows and special outings we went on but not others. He knew we'd travelled, but he'd forgotten a great deal of it. He said he knew we'd visited Fiji a few times, because he remembered the boat we took to the little island and that one time we rode in the helicopter to the island. He said that he was trying to remember the island itself and where we stayed, but he couldn't. I described it for him, but no matter how much I elaborated or what I described, his memory of it was gone.

Initially, he was concerned, but by this time he was just beginning to accept that he couldn't remember some things. I always reassured him that I still had our memories. I was keeping those memories now for both of us.

Geoffrey preferred to do as much as he could do himself. I let him, but it was emotionally tough to watch his struggles. When I offered to help, he would sometimes allow me to assist. More often than not, he would struggle on. I only got concerned when it looked like he was going to break something—for example, when he was pushing and pushing on something which only needed to be gently pulled.

Geoffrey told me that some mornings, he would wake up and not know where he was. He felt that he was supposed to get up and go home. Then he realised that he *did* live here. He shook off that weird feeling, as he called it, and then he was OK. Although I was very pleased that he was able to remember that he lived here, I also saw a possible glimpse of the future.

7

October 2017 turned out to be heart month.

Geoffrey turned 86. He had a lovely birthday, going on the usual Thursday bus trip with the Alzheimer's Australia Out and About Group. Thank goodness, he was enjoying these trips. He was now used to the routine and the people. I baked a cake and sent it with him, and he really enjoyed it. He was too tired for anything else that day, so we had a light dinner and were off to bed early. Everything seemed OK—or rather, there was nothing out of the ordinary.

Then, over the next few weeks, he began to get breathless. Even a short walk—and I mean very short, just to the car—and he was out of breath. He stopped wanting to get out of the car when we went anywhere; instead, he waited in the car, so I did the running around.

It was mid-October, on a rainy Sunday morning, when Geoffrey woke me at 3.30 a.m. He was very breathless and felt as if it was too hard to breathe. He'd been awake for an hour, and it was getting worse. I called an ambulance.

My youngest daughter and her family were staying with us that weekend, so I told them what was happening, and I went in the ambulance with Geoffrey to the local hospital. The emergency department in any hospital is busy on a Saturday night/Sunday morning, and I knew that this process was going to take ages. His vital signs were monitored, ECG done, cannula inserted, X-ray taken, blood taken.

Geoffrey couldn't give the doctor much info regarding his history, so I filled in the gaps, and the doctors arranged to get his medical records emailed from the two Melbourne hospitals where Geoffrey had had his surgery and post-surgery procedures.

Then we waited and waited. The nurses were wonderful people; the doctors were great. Everyone explained everything very well. Strange as it may seem, I didn't feel stressed or worried, just tired.

Eventually, Geoffrey was admitted to the medical assessment unit. At seven in the morning, I was told that the unit doctor would see him sometime after eight thirty or nine. I went home to get some breakfast, shower, and see my beautiful grandchildren.

I returned in time to be there when the unit doctor arrived. Geoffrey couldn't remember why he had gone to hospital in the first place, and many times when the doctor asked him something, I'd have to give the opposite answer because Geoffrey was unable to recall many health details correctly. He was being kept in overnight. I went home very late in the afternoon to find that Fiona had cooked dinner for everyone. How lovely! Oh, thank you, Fiona. I love you, Fi.

The family went home after dinner that Sunday night. I slept well and returned to the hospital in time for the morning doctor's review. Again, Geoffrey wanted to tell the doctor about things that had no relevance to his health but was unable to answer anything much about his body, his symptoms, or his feelings. He was discharged with a number of new medications which I would handle for him.

I still felt no stress. I had a kind of peaceful, comfortable knowing that everything was just as it was meant to be. I didn't have to push to get our needs met, nor did I need to worry. I was most definitely tired, but I did not feel overwhelmed. I felt supported by family and the hospital staff. Geoffrey's heart was, without a doubt, struggling. Surprisingly, I felt fine.

I sent a short email to friends and family to let them know what was going on. Many loving replies also helped me to feel well supported and cared for.

Over the next few weeks, Geoffrey showed small signs of heart failure—short breathless times, inability to walk very far, dozing in the chair often. In general, his energy levels were low, and he had another short stay in hospital after some breathlessness one night about ten days after the previous admission.

The cardiologist performed some more tests, which showed Geoffrey's heart's mitral valve was leaking. The original aortic valve replacement from 2014 had, from the beginning, a small leak also. Knowing that there were two leaking valves in his heart at least gave us a real reason for his problems. The cardiologist recommended an angiogram in order to see exactly what was going on and to maybe correct some problems.

A few days later, we were at the doctor's surgery to have a follow-up visit with our lovely GP. While we were waiting, a message came on my phone from the hospital asking me to call them to organise a pre-admission interview. Geoffrey glared at the phone and asked, "Who was that?" I told him what it was and said I'd call them when we got home. Geoffrey suggested that we just call in to the hospital on the way home. I explained that they just wanted me to phone them; we didn't need to go in. He became irritated and said that the hospital was not far and we should just call in on the way home.

The Gold Coast University Hospital was *huge*, the parking was expensive, and I had no idea where the particular unit I had to call was. It was no use trying to explain that, because logic doesn't work, so I was a bit stumped momentarily.

I took a breath and said to him, "OK, the GP is running a little late today, so we'll just see how much time we have after we've seen her.

We don't want to get stuck in the afternoon traffic." I was hoping that by then he'd have forgotten about it.

But no! As we were leaving and getting into the car, he started up again. "We'll call in to the hospital on the way home, won't we?"

"No," I said. "I'm tired. Let's just go home and have a cuppa, and I'll just phone the hospital."

His reply was, "Oh, OK. Are you sure?"

I breathed deeply and reassured him that it would be just fine. After a short while, he accepted that a cup of tea at home was probably a good idea.

Unfortunately, when Geoffrey was admitted to the Gold Coast University Hospital for the angiogram, the results were not favourable. We had hoped that maybe a stent might restore some blood flow if an artery was blocked. Perhaps they could have done a repair on the mitral valve. Either of these things would have helped him. Instead, they discovered that one artery was fully blocked (it had created its own little bypass) and the mitral valve was quite calcified and also quite close to a number of smaller arteries. In short, it was irreparable and too risky to try.

The symptoms of Geoffrey's heart disease were to be controlled with medication. This meant that I became the manager of his medications. He was still OK to take his supplements, because he'd been on them a long time and remembered what he needed to take. Plus, I wrote on the top of each container the quantity and the times he needed to take them, and I also kept an eye on him as he did this. Because most of the pharmaceutical medications were tiny pills, I also had to ensure that he didn't drop them. His hands were becoming increasingly shaky.

In general, I felt that I was handling Geoffrey's physical and cognitive problems better. I did find, though, that I was feeling increasingly lonely. It was simply because I could no longer have the little conversations we used to be able to have.

The truth was now impossible to ignore. Geoffrey's health was deteriorating on many facets. When I put my practical cap on, I had to be real about what I could and could not manage. For example, I could no longer manage the garden all by myself. Blue Care came to the rescue there. I organised a once-a-month gardener to come and trim back bushes, keep weeds away, and re-mulch the garden.

Thinking longer term, I knew I had to put something else in place. The reality was that we needed to downsize. I felt sad about leaving my beautiful home, even though I knew it would be the best and most sensible thing to do.

Every Thursday, after my art class and before Geoffrey was brought home from his bus trip, I looked at apartments. First of all, I checked out a couple of retirement places, but I quickly dismissed them as not suitable for me, and the weekly rates were far too expensive. I looked at a number of developments and off-the-plan apartments. I did not tell Geoffrey that I was doing this. I would tackle that later.

Some places offered a great deal, looked lovely, had high-quality finishes, and were close to the beach. *How great that would be*, I thought at first. Then I realised that year-round there'd be holiday-makers in a large number of the apartments, plus the body-corporate fees were high.

I moved the search closer to where we were currently living. Unfortunately, I discovered that all the apartment buildings were what I thought to be way too close to each other—I didn't want to be able to look across to someone else's balcony and be able to see exactly what they were having for breakfast, never mind the inevitable noise factor—or I considered the quality of the build and inclusions to be poor. One place looked good, but the position was way too noisy, as it was right next to the train line.

I felt the weight of responsibility heavily. Part of me was very confident in looking for something on my own. The other part felt sad and alone. I knew that Geoffrey could not traipse around looking at places, nor could he really be of any help in decision-making. I knew I'd have to choose my words and my attitude carefully when I broached the topic with him because he just *loved* our current home.

When looking for an apartment, I took into consideration a number of factors. I would have to feel comfortable there on my own and be able to manage physically and financially. It would have to be suitable for Geoffrey's increasing needs: no steps, easy access, walk-in shower, and so forth. At this stage, I had to plan for both—if Geoffrey was still with me and if he was not. Emotionally, this was tough. I kept reminding myself that I was always looked after and that I had to just trust.

My search continued. Eventually, I listened to my intuition (took me a while!) and went to the showroom of a new development about ten minutes north of our place. I had passed it every week on my way to art, and I had not looked there because I had not considered that area at all. Of course, it was perfect. A north-facing seventh-floor apartment with high-quality finishes, 2 large bedrooms, a small study, a view to the hills, two car spaces, and a lock-up space was the one I fell in love with. I could have my two little dogs on the understanding that when they passed, I could replace only one if I wanted another pet.

The development had a beautiful expansive pool and entertaining area with quality outdoor furniture, barbeques, sinks, benches, a gym, a sauna, and more. With already three buildings on the site spaced well away from each other, this apartment block was due to be finished between January 2020 and June 2020. This would give me two years to get our house in order and sell it in late 2019 or early 2020. I was still a little apprehensive about making this decision on my own. I breathed deeply a couple of times, and then I paid a holding deposit.

That evening, I broached the topic with Geoffrey. I told him I'd been checking out a few places and that I thought I'd found something really good. I strongly emphasised that it was *me* who couldn't cope with the big house and garden. Geoffrey was quite animated and thought it was a good idea for the future, and he could see that he wasn't up to doing as much as he used to. At this stage, though, he was still thinking that he was getting better and would be able to do more soon.

I felt vaguely guilty that I hadn't been 100 per cent honest with him. I had been told, though, that with him having dementia, I needed to lie sometimes in order to best manage his disease. It still wasn't a comfortable thing for me.

Next morning, I suggested that we go over the sales office, and I could show him the place and the show apartment to see what he thought. We visited that afternoon, and Geoffrey was smitten. He thought the apartments were lovely and that we should seriously think about it. So, we "thought" about it over the weekend. This meant that I brought the topic up a few times in a positive light. By Monday, I said that I was going to put a deposit on the apartment, and he was happy with this. I breathed a sigh of relief. That week I paid the full deposit, saw my conveyancer, and signed the full contract.

I had checked with an acquaintance who worked in the industry about the viability and reputation of both the developer and the builders before paying the full deposit. He had only good things to say about both. I felt comfortable to move forward.

We told everyone and showed family and friends the plans and brochures we had. I felt more secure in that I wouldn't have my children worrying about me managing a big house on my own. I felt really good knowing that I'd made the right decision. As the apartment was not going to be finished until at least early 2020, I still had plenty of time to enjoy our current beautiful home. That felt good.

8

Christmas 2017 was a quiet one. Phone calls from some of our kids was our only outside contact. I made us a nice roast turkey dinner and a plum pudding dessert. Geoffrey was fairly happy. I swam in the pool and had a fairly easy day.

My lovely friend Lyn had some of her family up from Melbourne, and they kindly offered to have us come over for Christmas lunch, but Geoffrey was not very good that week and I knew that he would not have handled it well. I unfortunately felt I had to decline the offer. It was for the best.

Geoffrey was spending a great deal of time sleeping. Snoozing in his chair was the usual thing. Often, he would turn on the television only to sleep in front of it.

Fiona and her family came down from the Sunshine Coast for my birthday (and my grandson's seventh birthday on the same day) and New Year. For the first time in many years, Geoffrey surprised me with a birthday gift. He had asked one of our lovely care workers to take him shopping one morning when I was not home in order to purchase something for me. That was sweet of him for sure.

Overall, it was a pretty good weekend. However, once again, I found that Geoffrey did not cope well with the noise and constant movement of the children. I did my best to manage him, but I could see that he was glad when they all went home.

The exterior house painting didn't get very far. It was only done for two weekends, then nothing for weeks and weeks. Fiona then left the marriage, and I understood completely and supported her fully. I knew that I'd just save up and get the rest of house painted before it was sold. No big deal. I suppose that I could have felt let down, but instead, I felt happy that Fiona was doing what she needed to do for herself.

———◆———

By February 2018, there were many little things that showed Geoffrey's slow but steady deterioration. He was becoming more and more anxious about time. *What time is it? What time do we have to leave? What time do we have to be there? Come on, we won't have time! What time will this or that happen?* And many more such questions every single day.

His short-term memory was also getting worse. He would become very grumpy and rude, saying that I hadn't told him about something. Of course, I had informed him. He'd forgotten, so I told him again—and again and again sometimes. Very tiring for me, I can tell you.

Geoffrey seemed to be more and more dissatisfied and more critical of everything, and he did not want to put any effort into anything. The only exception was the meals I made for him. He was, for the most part, very happy with what I cooked. I knew that his back gave him a bit of pain, but I couldn't get him to take any painkillers. So he grumbled about other things, he snoozed, he ate, he snoozed, he grumbled. And we went on like this.

———◆———

By now, a higher level of home care package (level 3) had come through, and I did enjoy my time off when he had a care worker and also when he went on his Thursday bus trips. I especially enjoyed my "to myself time" since I wasn't using these days to apartment-hunt any more. I can't say that I was really stressed, because I just took things a day at a time.

I was often overwhelmed and a bit sad or lonely. At those times, I asked myself, "What am I making matter?" I reminded myself that what was going on now was just how it was. Without any judgement, it just was how it was. I gave myself time to go into another room, go for a short walk, chat on the phone to a friend, or have a swim. Then I felt better.

It did become difficult to do, however, when Geoffrey's heart problems and dementia combined with his increasing hearing loss. Geoffrey's need for everything to be regular and routine worked fine in theory, but in real life, things changed. Sometimes it was me who needed a change.

An example was breakfast time We would usually have either cereal or boiled eggs with toast and a cup of tea. Geoffrey used to help with the preparation. He would boil the kettle and make the tea, or he would get crockery and cutlery out of the drawers, or he would get what was needed from the pantry. Now we were at a stage where he very rarely did anything. He'd sit down and wait for his breakfast to be put in front of him; only occasionally would he actually do anything to get breakfast happening.

One morning, I decided to have fried eggs on toast for a change. I prepared what was needed: put the toast in the toaster, made the tea, put cutlery on the table, and so on. As it was cooking, Geoffrey got out the condiments for toast. I told him we didn't need them because I was doing fried eggs.

"Oh," he replied.

I took the small tray with the honey, peanut butter, etc., and placed it back into the pantry. I put the jam back into the fridge.

Suddenly he roared at me, "What are you doing? I got that out. We need it for breakfast."

"I'm making *fried* eggs," I repeated.

He became very agitated and yelled at me to "Just serve my breakfast!"

I took a deep breath as I plated up the food. I put his plate in front of him and snapped, "Your breakfast is served, sir."

He looked at it and blinked. Somewhat sheepishly, he said, "Well, I didn't know what you were making for breakfast!"

I just sighed. He hadn't heard me. His hearing aids were not in his ears yet. It was a lethal combination: dementia, which meant an inability to process what was going on around him, creating a total lack of awareness, plus deafness with no hearing aids. If he had been normal, he would have seen and noticed what I was making. Oh, how easy life used to be!

It was the hundreds of little things like the breakfast debacle which made everyday life so difficult. It didn't help that in the mornings, he'd refuse to put his hearing aids in until he was 100 per cent sure that his ears were dry from his morning shower. Of course, he allowed masses more time than was actually needed to dry his ears. I'd either get ignored because he hadn't heard me or end up having to repeat and repeat what I'd said until I was shouting. Then he'd get cross because I was shouting at him.

I'd tell him that I refused to talk to him in the mornings until his hearing aids were in. But I knew that by the next morning, he would have forgotten I'd said that.

One day, just as I was about to make us a cup of tea, I noticed that Geoffrey had kindly put the mugs out and had placed a teabag into one of the mugs. (We usually share a tea bag, as we like our tea weak black.) I did a double-take as I noticed the mugs were dirty. Geoffrey was having what I thought was a good day, and he was in the midst of emptying the dishwasher. I placed the dirty mugs on top of the bench near the dishwasher and turned to take a couple of clean ones from the drawer—only to find that they were also dirty.

"Hang on a minute," I said. "What are you doing?" It dawned on me that Geoffrey was busy emptying the dirty dishes out of the dishwasher. I immediately stopped him from removing any more soiled plates from the lower shelf, and I pointed out that they were dirty too, as the dishwasher had not been turned on yet that day.

I took a breath. He hadn't noticed. He'd seen a fairly full load and assumed it needed emptying. He didn't see, didn't notice, wasn't aware that the mugs, glasses, and cooking utensils he'd put away were still dirty.

I took another breath as Geoffrey started a ramble about how he wasn't aware and that he was just trying to help. I thanked him and proceeded to go through all the crockery, cutlery, and so forth in order to place what was dirty into the dishwasher again, plus a few extra things which had become soiled from the whole process. I turned the dishwasher on and returned to making the tea.

I could see that he was becoming sheepish and felt bad that he'd done the wrong thing. So I jollied him out of it. "Do you think we need to have a funeral?" I asked him with a big smile. When he asked what for, I replied laughingly, "Well, it looks like awareness has died. Maybe we'll just need to have a memorial service instead?" I laughed and added, "How could you not see that those were dirty dishes? You are hilarious!"

"Oh well," he smiled. "I might need new glasses, hey?"

"Will we get your new glasses before or after the awareness funeral?" I asked.

He tutted at me good-heartedly, giggled, and went on with his crossword puzzle. Disaster averted!

But yes, awareness was dead, or dying anyway, gone down the same path as logic, swallowed up by this thing called dementia.

———————◆———————

I'd spend time preparing dinner in the kitchen (which was open-plan with the family room where Geoffrey was sitting). As dinner was cooking away, either on the stove-top or in the oven, Geoffrey would ask me if I was going to make dinner tonight.

Other times, he'd call out, "My hearing aid batteries have run out again. That's strange. You just put new batteries in yesterday, didn't you?"

No, I had replaced the batteries a full six days prior. They always lasted six days, and I would put fresh batteries in every six days.

"I've lost my glasses!" he'd roar.

Would that be them sitting on the table beside you?

"I need drops in my eyes. I haven't had any drops in my eyes for weeks," Geoffrey would proclaim loudly.

I put drops into Geoffrey's eyes *every* morning!

"When are you going to phone to get a physio appointment for me?"

Geoffrey had been sitting at the table twenty minutes earlier when I sat right next to him making that exact appointment.

"What have you done with the TV remote? I can't find it!" he'd call out.

Would that be it on your lap?

And best of all: I told him that I had done two loads of washing and that I was going to hang it all out on the line. I repeated that it was *two* loads and that I'd be a while. I asked if he needed anything and said yet again that I was going out back to hang the washing. I even asked him if he knew what I was about to do, and he snapped that of course he had heard me and that I was going to hang washing. He added that he was not stupid and that he understood perfectly well.

So out I went. I hung up all the clothes as fast as I could. When I came back inside, I went from the laundry into the kitchen, and I couldn't see Geoffrey. Then I heard him up the other end of the house. He was looking for me.

"Where are you?" he called.

I called back that I was in the kitchen.

He grumbled as he came back down the hall towards me, "Where have you been?"

When I told him that I'd been hanging out the washing, he snapped, "Well, you could have told me."

"Oh, silly me," I replied. "I should have told you."

I could go on and on with masses of little things, all of which were funny, but many of which became overwhelming and frustrating.

———◆———

In the mornings, I'd give Geoffrey all of his medications. Because I'd write the dosage on the lid of each of his supplements—one in morning, two morning and night, and so on—so far, he was able manage to take his supplements himself. In the evenings, though, there was a quarter of a tablet which was a medication, and I usually cut the pill into quarters in the pill cutter. There were always a few quarters in the pill-cutter tray. Geoffrey would get his quarter himself at night, although I always checked that he'd had it.

One evening, I noticed that he was having difficulty getting the quarter tab out of the container. "Would you like some help" I asked. But no, he was determined to do it himself, so I left him to it.

A minute went by. I looked up, and he was still fiddling with the container. He licked his finger and stuck it into the well of the container containing the quarter tablet pieces.

"Stop!" I called out. I jumped up and attempted to stop him from dipping his licked finger in again. "Don't put your spit into it," I said firmly.

"I didn't," Geoffrey protested.

Oh my God, I thought. *He's just like a child!*

I said to him, "You licked your finger and put it into the container. Now look what you've done. All the pieces are squashed and falling apart; you've wet them all. That's disgusting!" I took the container away from him, tipped the soggy and crumbling pieces into the bin, and washed the pill cutter/container.

All the while, Geoffrey was standing there yelling at me. First came the childish excuses: "I couldn't get it out. I've gotten them out like that before. You don't understand. It was OK." Then the attacks: "You always have to be right. You can't keep your nose out of things. You always interfere. You're a perfectionist. You are a real nuisance. You don't understand. I know what I'm doing; you don't. Just let me do it. I'm OK. I don't need any of your interfering!"

I could not shut him up, so I reacted. I knew it was not the best thing to do, but sometimes it became so overwhelming. I was so sick and tired of having him acting like a child. It was bedtime, and I was tired. I took my pillow from our bed and went to sleep in another room. I just couldn't bear to be near him.

But oh dear—that was probably the worst thing I could have done. Five minutes later, he was roaring for me to come to bed. I ignored him. He eventually came into the room I'd moved to and wanted to start all his reasons and excuses and attacks all over again. I told him I didn't want to talk about it anymore. I told him to go to bed.

He wanted to know why I was sleeping there and not in our bed. That just made it worse for me. I was *so* cross that he was being a child.

Eventually he went back to bed, and I had a good night's sleep on my own.

In the morning, I remembered that I never did give him his quarter pill the night before.

9

It was early March 2018, and I was getting things organised for me to go to Melbourne for eight days. I had arranged for Geoffrey to go into residential respite while I was away. The aged care facility had a two-week minimum respite stay requirement, so I had to pay for two full weeks whether we used it or not. I decided that I would pick Geoffrey up in the afternoon of day 12 (the third day after I returned home), hoping that would give me some time to myself after a busy trip. He wanted me to arrange to pick him up on the evening I returned. I said no. Day 12 instead of the full two weeks was the compromise.

As the time came closer, he became increasingly anxious about going into respite care. We had talked a lot about him not being able to come to Melbourne with me and that respite care was the only sensible option. I knew he understood, but I could also understand his anxiety around it all. It was all new. He had never been an overly sociable fellow, and being faced with so many strangers around him was a bit scary.

I offered to take him for a visit so that he could look around, and he agreed it would be a good idea. We visited and were shown one of the rooms so that Geoffrey could see how big they were and see all the facilities in the room and around the whole place. We met some of the lovely staff and saw the activities program. He settled somewhat after the visit, thank goodness!

In preparation for Geoffrey's residential respite, I had to name all his clothes and personal items. Iron-on labels worked fine for his clothes. I used a Dymo labeller for other things. Mostly that worked, but for some items, a permanent marker was needed.

One morning whilst in the ensuite, Geoffrey was growling about some stupid thing and kept telling me that "the name's come up on the phone". As he did not have a mobile phone and mine was in the bedroom, I initially had no idea what he was talking about. Once he turned around and I saw that he was shaking his razor, I realised that he meant that the name label had come *off* his *razor.* When I voiced that, he snapped, "That's what I said!"

I just had to stay patient. He had no idea that he had not explained himself well. The white permanent marker did a good job on it. It was named well and could not come off.

⬧•❖•⬧

I had purchased from the audiologist a Bluetooth device which hooked up to the television and transmitted the audio directly into Geoffrey's hearing aids. Whilst he was using this, I could turn down the volume of the television, which was a godsend. It was making *me* deaf that he would constantly want the television turned up on high volume. Better still, I could even mute it altogether, and Geoffrey could still hear the television loud and clear directly through his hearing aids. It took a bit of fiddling to get set up, but once it was sorted, it worked wonderfully well.

One evening, Geoffrey started to grumble that it wasn't working. I knew the problem wasn't his hearing aids, as I had just replaced the batteries in them that morning. He was continuing to grumble about "the damn thing doesn't work" while he attempted to bash his hearing aid remote control on the arm of the chair in order to make it function. All that I saw was Geoffrey trying to, yet again, break something.

Once I took the hearing aid remote control from him, I checked that the batteries were in properly. Often, he would drop this small remote, the back would open, and the batteries would dislodge. Sometimes Geoffrey would put them back in properly and sometimes not. I established that it all looked OK.

He was still grumbling about "the damn thing's not working, and I've checked it all, and you won't find anything wrong. It's not working. I can't hear anything at all!"

I glanced up at him and noticed that his hearing aids were not even in his ears. "No wonder you can't hear anything!" I said. I laughed and called him a silly old bugger, and he laughed too. It was very funny. He gave me his hearing aids from his pocket, and I put them in for him. Funnily enough, he could then hear the TV!

I found myself really enjoying these "normal" moments when we could laugh together, usually at something silly that had occurred. These times were becoming more and more rare, and they were precious moments indeed.

Geoffrey was often having problems with his hearing aids. For example, he would get frustrated and annoyed that one or the other of the hearing aids was not working, only to find that the battery had fallen out and was still in his pocket or on the floor. Throughout each fiasco of me attempting to fix the situation, Geoffrey would protest that the hearing aid was working earlier or that he'd put them in properly, or that I should just get new batteries and put them in. Sometimes he would be grumpy about it; occasionally, he would be good-humoured.

There were a number of incidents prior to Geoffrey going into respite care, and I found that I was stretched to the limit of my patience. I knew that I really needed some time away, and I was very glad that he was not coming with me to Melbourne. I felt a little guilty about being happy to leave him. Nevertheless, I seriously need some time to myself.

I left Geoffrey at the residential respite care home. It honestly looked like a like a six-star resort. I knew he was not all that happy for me to leave him there, but he accepted that to travel to Melbourne and to keep up with all my appointments would be much too difficult for him. I knew he was in good hands and that he'd be looked after just fine.

Turns out I wasn't totally correct about that. The first night, I received a phone call from the care home. There was a problem with Geoffrey's medications. I didn't understand how that could be—our GP had filled in all the forms, writing up both his medications and his complementary supplements. The pharmacist had packed it all into a Webster pack. All the nurse had to do was give him everything that was in the Webster pack.

On the phone to me, they stated that because they did not have a full description of every supplement, they did not know what they were giving him, and therefore they could not give him anything. The fact that Geoffrey was not able to identify which pills or tablets were which did not help the situation. I, being in Melbourne by then, was horrified. I had gone to a great deal of trouble to ensure his medications and the supplements were all packed according to how the home had requested.

It took several calls that evening before they would give him at least his pharmaceutical medications. The next day, and many calls later—including calls to our GP and one of her reception staff—it was finally sorted. I had a busy schedule for the Melbourne trip, and it was a very stressful way to begin.

I phoned Geoffrey most nights, and he usually was fine, but every day he found something to complain about. I stayed cheery and tried to encourage him to participate in some of the many and varied activities available to him. As it turned out, he did not participate in anything the whole time he was there. He went to the dining room for lunch and dinner, and that was it. He stayed in his room other than that. I know that was his choice, but I found it frustrating that I had found a beautiful place for him with many choices of activities and that I had paid extra to have everything available for him, and he'd opted to use none of it.

Geoffrey was glad to be home when I collected him. He was really nice to me for about a week. Then Mr Grumpy returned.

10

Geoffrey was, at this stage, becoming confused with his supplements, so I took over not just his medications, which I had been doing for a while, but his supplements as well. It was far easier for me to do it all than to deal with questions each day about what he should be taking.

I found it difficult not to become frustrated when Geoffrey would be in the kitchen trying to help with something. He would take a long time to do simple tasks. On a rational level, I totally understand that his brain was not functioning in a normal way, and it took a while for his thought processes to work through doing whatever task he decided to help with. Sometimes he would just be standing in the middle of the kitchen not moving in any direction, and as I tried to get past him, I had to take care not to knock him or he could lose his balance.

I had no idea what he was doing sometimes or if he was about to move in one direction or another. If I asked him, he'd get annoyed and just grump at me to give him time. When I had already waited several minutes to see what he was doing or where he was going, I had to breathe very deeply and wait some more until he actually moved out of my way.

He was becoming more and more grumpy and short-tempered. I dealt with this by spending some time locked away in the office at the front of the house while Geoffrey watched TV. When I had some privacy, I phoned one of the dementia help lines. I found that talking to someone who understood enabled me to get it out, and I was able to regain a better perspective once again. Then I felt like I could cope.

A visit to the GP and some routine tests revealed that Geoffrey had a UTI. A course of antibiotics seemed to do the trick, and his better-humoured self returned!

Before too long, however, he was back to Mr Grumpy. He had no energy at all and wanted to sleep a lot. Turned out he had another UTI, so more antibiotics followed. As he didn't seem to have any symptoms other than being grumpy, it was hard to tell if he was just deteriorating in general or if he was unwell with another UTI.

Because Geoffrey was just not able to think logically, he would become cross with me. One day, I unlocked the car and got into the driver's seat. Geoffrey was not yet in the car. He was rattling the door handle, and it wouldn't open. What had happened was that he had started to pull on the handle just as I had unlocked it, so his door did not release and was still locked. He pulled and rattled the door, and I called out to him through the closed door to let the handle go so that I could unlock his door. He just kept pulling and rattling the unlocked door, becoming more and more cross. I yelled very loudly so that he could hear me, instructing him to just let go of the handle for a moment.

He eventually did let go, and I was able to unlock the door. Geoffrey got into the car and harrumphed at me, "God, you're hard to live with!"

I was so annoyed that I snapped, "*I'm* hard to live with? You're not so dammed easy to live with yourself!" The rest of the trip was uneventful—and quiet!

———◆·◆·◆———

It was essential to have help with some of the general things around the house, because I found that I was unable to do it all as well as keep an eye on Geoffrey and in general take care of him. Blue Care was organising some help with the garden, but it seemed to take ages, and the gardening people did not always come when they had previously arranged to come. The bushes and hedges were overgrown, the grass was long, and our lovely mowing man was on holidays.

Every time Geoffrey looked outside at the back garden, he would comment on how bad it looked. He was becoming annoyed by it and frustrated that he couldn't do anything about it. All I could do was make phone calls and attempt to organise the gardeners to come. Eventually they did, and Geoffrey was relieved. So was I.

My old frustration returned each time I attempted to assist Geoffrey with something. He was insistent that he was all right to walk short distances without his wheelie-walker. He would, for example, leave the walker next to the driver's side of the car, and he'd walk around to the passenger side and get into the car. I knew he was doing this to help me, because I would put the walker in behind the driver's seat. What he wouldn't acknowledge was that it was dangerous for him, as his balance was very bad. He'd wobble from side to side as he stabilized himself by holding on to the car all the way around.

When I said to him that he could take the walker right around to his door and I would then wheel it around put it into the car, he just grumped at me and said, "I'm OK. I know what I'm doing! Just leave it and stop fussing!"

I was concerned and worried that he'd fall. I knew the consequences of this would be considerable, and I had no idea how to get this through to him. Part of me knew, however, that getting something logical through to him would be impossible.

Worry is a waste of energy. I know this.

Our thoughts carry an energy, just as everything has an energy. Worrying has absolutely no positive benefit for anyone. Worry just ties up our brain and takes away our inner peace. It puts us into a powerless place and puts our energy into something negative rather than into peace, allowance, and is-ness. This means that Geoffrey is how he is, and it is not my place to make him any different.

INSIGHT - SIX

When we worry, we are allowing ourselves to be consumed about what-ifs and things out of our control. Worry can lead to taking an excessive amount of responsibility for things that we cannot actually control. This leads to a feeling of powerlessness, and then frustration or anger can take over.

It is useless to try to take responsibility for someone else. We only need to take responsibility for ourselves. We can assist. We can support. Ultimately, though, it is for each one of us to take responsibility for ourselves.

Even though Geoffrey was no longer 100 per cent capable of logical thought, I was only making things difficult for myself if I took over responsibility for him. All I needed to do was take care of his needs and do the best I could to keep his environment as safe as possible.

11

Just when things seemed to be going relatively smoothly, the Gold Coast hosted the Commonwealth Games. It was widely publicised that Gold Coasters should expect a huge increase in traffic and that either going away for holidays or staying off the roads as much as possible was advised.

The reality was somewhat different. The roads were extremely quiet unless you went close to any of the venues. The Coast was as devoid of traffic as I or anyone had ever seen, and getting around had never been easier. Many businesses had decided not to open for those two weeks, and a huge number of Gold Coasters took holidays away.

Unfortunately, Geoffrey's bus trip was cancelled for those two weeks. Our Blue Care package manager organised a care worker for those Thursday mornings from an agency so that I could still attend my art classes. I came home from art class on the first Thursday and immediately saw that our garage door had been damaged—quite dented and scratched. Turns out the agency care worker had backed into the garage door. The door was still working, but the damage was obvious.

Oh, great, I thought. *Another thing for me to sort out, think about, and organise!*

During this period, I was doing my best to tidy and begin to clear out cupboards and sort things. I have so many beautiful items that we have either bought or that I have been given, but I realised that when we moved into the apartment, I was not going to have anywhere near enough room for everything.

I tended to go through my things in stages. The first stage was to put items into the garage which I easily knew I could let go or live without. Some of these items were kitchen paraphernalia which had been in cupboards and left unused for the whole time we'd been in the current house. They were the easy things. Then I moved onto what I call the *stuff*.

The process became more difficult when I looked at many of our beautiful paintings, sculptures, crystals, and mementos. I knew that things are only things, and I was able to let go of many possessions because they were not what was truly precious in this life. I was not a hoarder by any means. I did have many items in my house which I did not necessarily need, but a great number of my things brought to mind happy times or memories of when we stretched ourselves financially to afford a special piece of art or were given something special by a group of friends.

I note here that I have used the word *special* a few times when describing things or possessions that I have had emotional attachments to because they remind me of those special times. I guess if I was being honest, it was times where love was tangible and in some way was expressed through an item.

As I started to go through more items in the house, I discovered that I had emotional attachments to a great number of things. I was slowly losing Geoffrey, and removing some of the things we particularly chose and purchased together was difficult. I was feeling cautious about not losing too much all at once.

I stopped sorting and clearing out. I knew it needed to be done. *Just not yet*, I thought. It wasn't fun!

Insight – Seven

Possessions are just things. It is not things which matter in this life; it is our heartfelt connections, our love, our sense of adventure, our laughter, peace, and joy. It is so easy to become attached to things because of the memories each piece may evoke.

In truth, if we are at peace within ourselves, value ourselves, and know love, we have no real need for lots of things. In our society, though, we like to decorate our houses and surround ourselves with lovely things.

This way, when it comes time to let go of some of the items, decorations, and possessions from our homes, it is not a loss; it is generosity. We can experience a great deal of fulfillment because we are giving someone joy or the potential for joy from the item. This is especially true when it is something we have loved and enjoyed greatly ourselves. It becomes a gift rather than a loss. In this way, uncluttering or thinning down our things can be fun.

Geoffrey became more and more cranky. I was getting stressed to the max. He was very difficult with everything. Then we discovered that he had another UTI. I'd had no idea. He did not have any of the usual symptoms—no fever, no trouble urinating, no frequent urinating, no bladder discomfort, nothing! This time, it took three courses of antibiotics to clear it up.

By now, Geoffrey was no longer interested in doing anything work-related. He had always been the one to say that he never wanted to retire, that he loved our work and wanted to do it forever. Now, though, he never mentioned anything work-related at all. In fact, he didn't want to do anything much. He'd sit in the chair all day and snooze off and on, or watch TV, still snoozing off and on.

———◆———

By April, I found myself cleaning the bathroom floor a lot. Geoffrey would either start urinating before he sat down or, when standing, he would miss the toilet bowl completely. I found myself constantly reassuring him, because on the occasions he realised that he'd made a mess, he was most upset. He could also see that he was causing me extra work. There were, however, more occasions when he had no idea at all that he'd made a mess. Sometimes it was only when I commented on his wet trousers that he realised what had happened.

One Thursday, he returned from the usual bus trip and bolted to the en suite. He took a long time, and when I went in to see if he was OK, I discovered him desperately trying to get his wet pants and trousers off amid a sea of urine on the floor. I could see that he felt awful, and my heart went out to him. I felt a bit helpless when all I could do was reassure him, give him a wash, and get him into fresh clothes. This was something I couldn't fix for him. I did feel sad.

We had the "it might be a good idea to try a pad in your pants" conversation, as I clearly saw that the problem occurred more often when Geoffrey had left it too long to give himself time to get to the toilet. It was simply urge incontinence. To my surprise, he took it really well and agreed to give it a go. I bought large pads for men, and for a while, I thought that this was sorted.

The other physical thing that was occurring was Geoffrey's increased inability to mobilise very well. He was becoming slower and slower on his wheelie-walker. He was unable to walk more than twenty or thirty metres without stopping to sit down for a rest. He was finding it harder to get up from a chair. He would walk around the kitchen benches when he was in the kitchen and was unable to take many steps without holding on to something. When he did walk without holding anything, he was extremely wobbly. He wobbled from side to side and looked very unsteady indeed. His urine test came back negative, so at least it wasn't another UTI.

We continued, on good days, to have an old joke about how much we loved each other. I'd tell him that I loved him, and he would reply, "I love you too."

"Only two?" I'd ask, with a grin on my face.

He'd think a moment and sometimes say that he loved me nine, or twenty, or eighty-seven, or some other random number.

Sometimes I would query, "What about eleventy-seven? Do you love me eleventy-seven?"

We would usually end up saying that we loved each other *all* the numbers! Then we'd laugh.

One lunchtime, I took Geoffrey to have a Yum Cha lunch—it had always been one of his favourite lunchtime outings. In hindsight, I should have put his suggestion off until a weekday. This was a Saturday, and of course, the place was busy. Geoffrey struggled to walk in between the tables to get to our allocated table, the only empty one in the place. By the time he got to the table, he was exhausted, and he slumped onto the chair. Almost falling onto the floor and only half on the seat, he just couldn't manoeuvre his legs under the table or move himself fully onto the chair. He looked awkward and surely must've felt awkward.

We survived the meal, but Geoffrey managed to spill almost everything all over his shirt. It seemed that he no longer could manage chopsticks. I asked for a spoon and fork for him. Admittedly, the chairs were quite low, but I had to fully lift him up when it was time to go, in a restaurant full of people. I knew that he was uncomfortable by the way he tried to exit the place as fast as he could manage.

I realised afterward that he must have just been having a bad dementia day, because Geoffrey was able to manage his chopsticks the next time we went somewhere to have Asian food. I guess that is the nature of vascular dementia. Geoffrey could go down, so to speak, then pick up a little, but not usually to the full capacity of how he'd been previous to the going-down time.

***

Geoffrey had an ultrasound of his bladder, prostate, and kidneys, but when we went to the doctor to get the results, they hadn't sent them through. It was annoying, because the effort involved in getting Geoffrey to the radiographer and then on another day to the doctor was considerable.

He appeared to be fairly good, all things considered, and his mind seemed to clear a bit. Geoffrey's middle daughter, Vicki, came up from Melbourne to visit. She arrived on a Monday afternoon and left on Thursday early afternoon. During the time Vicki stayed, it was as if Geoffrey had swallowed a magic pill. He was bright, fairly on the ball cognitively, and good-humoured. Although it was wonderful to have him enjoying his visitor and fully participating in everything, it was also tough emotionally, because I was sure that Vicki thought I had been exaggerating her dad's symptoms and how much work everything was.

If I'm honest, it hurt a little when Vicki stated that her mum, in a care home in Melbourne, was more work and much more forgetful than Geoffrey. I did have to hold my tone steady as I replied that it is quite different when you are looking after someone 100 per cent of the time. I took a really big breath. I did realise that she was attempting to empathise with me by telling me how much worse her mum was, but I was feeling oversensitive.

Geoffrey was stable for a number of weeks, but when he next saw the cardiologist, his medication was increased. Geoffrey was sleeping a lot through the day, and he was very breathless with the least bit of exertion.

12

Mother's Day weekend 2018, we had Fiona and the children come down to stay from the Sunshine Coast. We all went to the farmers market on the Sunday morning. Usually it is an outing Geoffrey enjoys, but this time he found it very hard to get around. He spent a lot of the time just sitting on the seat of his wheelie-walker because he was too tired to walk as far as we were going.

The weather was beautiful, and after we had done all the shopping, we sat at a table in between the playground and the food stalls listening to the buskers' music as we kept an eye on the kids in the playground. Geoffrey rested. We bought breakfast and coffee and enjoyed the winter sun and the beautiful vista of parklands, lake, and a nice view of the city (Surfers Paradise). Geoffrey enjoyed the view and loved to just people-watch. I could see that he was quite tired, but as the children were happy to play, we stayed a fair while.

The toilets were about a hundred metres away, so I made sure that we set off towards them before the need was too urgent for Geoffrey. We approached the facilities, and I had to point out the route he had to go in order to enter the men's. When he came out, he looked somewhat confused, and I needed to point out where the handwashing facilities were. As it was ultra-modern, he was looking quite puzzled at the basins with no taps in sight. I demonstrated how to use them (automatic sensor), and then he was fine.

As we slowly made our way away from the men's room, I could see why I was always tired. It was the mental requirement to keep one step ahead of what he might need, one step ahead of what he might not understand anymore, one step ahead of everything that might cause confusion or stress for him. The constant on-alert state of mind reminded me of when I had young children and had to be on alert all the time because they would get into goodness knows what mischief. It was a different scenario, but the feeling was the same. I was in my twenties when I had small children, and I was still full of energy myself. I was in my sixties now. Big difference!

After that outing, Geoffrey slept most of the rest of the day.

———————

I was thinking that a mobility scooter might help Geoffrey enjoy outings a little more. Just a couple of weeks prior to this, I had chatted with a gentleman in the supermarket who I saw had a very nifty mobility scooter. He had told me that it went well on gravel or grass and up and down inclines. It folded up to go in the car. He and his wife had travelled overseas with his mobility scooter, and it was not much bigger than carry-on luggage. I decided that it was now time I looked into this.

Over the next week, I looked online and in person at showrooms. I found there to be a great number of mobility scooters, many of which came apart and could be put into the boot of the car. In the showrooms, I could only find one type that folded up, but it did not seem as robust or as powerful to keep going up inclines as the one that the gentleman in the supermarket had had. I made enquiries about it and found a demo model of the exact same type and model. We ended up purchasing that one, and thankfully, there was enough money in Geoffrey's home care package to pay for it.

I had to make it an exciting thing in order for Geoffrey to agree to use a mobility scooter. I had to come up with all sorts of ideas and places we could go and he could use it and not get as tired as he was becoming when he used his wheelie-walker. I could see that he was a bit reluctant, because he was frightened that he might not be able to work it. Over and over, I reassured him that we could practice with it a lot before he went anywhere. We got the mobility scooter. It is called a Luggie.

It did take considerable time and practice for Geoffrey to get the hang of riding the Luggie. The controls were very simple: In front of the handles was a toggle bar. Grab the right side and squeeze towards the handlebar, and it moves forward. Let it go, and the Luggie stops. Grab the left side and squeeze towards the handlebar, and it moves backwards. Let either of the toggles go, and the Luggie stops. There's a dial which controls the speed from very slow up to a good fast pace. The handlebar turns just like a bike so that you can turn left or right. Sounds easy if you have all your faculties.

I took Geoffrey and the Luggie to an unused car park to practice. Of course, he kept getting cross with me. I was teaching him to use one side of the toggle at a time. He wanted to keep his fingers on the reverse toggle while going forward so that he could use it to brake. This was not a good idea, as if he slammed it into reverse before it had fully stopped, he could have jammed the poor motor. Getting him to trust that the vehicle would stop as soon as he released the toggle and then he could reverse if he wanted to was stressful for both of us.

Eventually, he got the hang of it, although he did forget to look and see what was behind him sometimes before he reversed, and he sometimes panicked when he was headed towards something and left it too late to let go of the toggle to stop. Consequently, he would bang into walls on occasions. This caused the battery to jump out of its slot, and then Geoffrey wondered why it wouldn't work. I'd turn the Luggie off, push the battery back into place, and all was well again. Each time it happened, he'd say with a grin, "Oops, I was going too fast, wasn't I?"

It took weeks, but eventually, Geoffrey mastered the Luggie fairly well. I just had to make sure he knew where to go. He was easily disoriented and could often head in the opposite or wrong direction to where we were meant to be going.

He enjoyed following me round the supermarket in the Luggie and enjoyed going for coffee where he could just ride up beside any of the outdoor tables. The farmers market was much more enjoyable for him having the freedom of the Luggie. He was up there with me at every stall, often making his own fruit choices and so on.

Just as the Luggie was beginning to bring Geoffrey easier mobility, but before he was confident with it, the staff from the Out and About Program bus trip he enjoyed every Thursday reported to their boss about Geoffrey's decreased mobility on his wheelie-walker. They told me about it, and I told them that Geoffrey was now fairly confident on the Luggie and that maybe he could use that on his Thursday bus trips. They said that they'd have to check with the boss.

A week later, I found myself having a conversation with the boss, only to discover that there was no way he would agree to Geoffrey taking or using a motorised scooter on the bus trips. He claimed that the staff were not trained in lifting techniques in order to get the scooter onto the bus. Even though I explained that it could to be lifted into the back of my car easily, there was no convincing him. Geoffrey had one more Thursday trip, and that was that.

The boss said that he would inform the staff and they would all be able to say goodbye to Geoffrey, as he'd been doing the bus trips for a long time now. He assured me that Geoffrey would be made a fuss of and have a great last day with them.

Emotionally, I went down a slippery slope. I was devasted. It had taken ages for Geoffrey to begin to enjoy his Thursday bus trips. At first, he had complained that it was all old people who went on the outings. I remember having to remind him that he was also an old person! Then he had become used to it. Then he had moved on to looking forward to the outings, and finally he was enjoying them immensely and liked appreciated the staff enormously. I loved my Thursday art classes, and I wouldn't think of not going anymore.

I felt as though one very big door had just smashed in my face. I was in the middle of nowhere, and I couldn't even see another door, never mind opening another one. *It's OK*, I told myself. *Something will turn up.* But my panic was palpable, as I had no idea how I was going to find something else in a week to ten days.

The boss had told me that our package manager should find something else for Geoffrey, but in reality, I knew how busy our home care package manager was, and I seriously doubted that he would have time to organise something else. I even questioned whether the package manager would even know what else was around that could work for us.

I just sat down and cried. My sensible self knew that I was always looked after and that something could be sorted, but right in that moment, I felt very let down and hopeless. I felt abandoned and uncared for. I felt the weight of the world on my shoulders, and I felt very alone.

After a good cry and a phone call to a friend, I pulled myself together and began to make phone calls to enquire as to what organisation might have something suitable. I was able to get back into the space of this being an opportunity. There must be something better around. I just did not know what it was right then.

———•:◆:•———

INSIGHT – EIGHT

The notion that we are always looked after is a feeling of trusting in God or a higher power or the universe or the essence of our soul. It is knowing that we are always brought to a place that is right for us or that the right thing will come to us when we take action with a loving, trusting heart.

Usually, in the past, we have reacted to events, and this has set a pattern or automatic response or reaction to what is currently occurring. When things have gone wrong in our lives or we've had challenges, we have learned to deal with them based on our upbringing, what we've seen others in society do, or from our child- or teen-self. This often comes from a place of just reacting with anger and blame.

Sometimes we hold on to a hard-done-by feeling for a long time, continuing to move through our lives constantly finding others to blame for our perceived misfortunes. Some of us become hardened to the world; we do what we can to be insular and never allow others to do anything for us. We find a way to fix everything ourselves. We can become bitter if we take the attitude that *I always have to do everything myself.*

In our Western society, we are encouraged to blame, as our society teaches us that there is always someone at fault. As such, we are encouraged to blame rather than consider some of the Eastern beliefs and philosophies which come from the perspective of taking personal responsibility. This means that everything happens for a reason and that every experience can teach us something.

When we are trusting and knowing that everything happens for a reason, we are more open to allowing help, assistance, and support. When something goes awry, we are willing to looking at the situation as an opportunity for learning or for change. Maybe it is just an opportunity to get back in touch with ourselves and to allow assistance from those who love us. Sometimes it is for reasons unknown. But when we hold on to the judgement that what has occurred is bad or *I have to do it all myself*, it is difficult for us to seek or receive help, assistance, and support.

Many people spend their whole lives moving from one drama to another, which keeps them feeling hard done by or victimised, never stopping to take responsibility for their own thoughts around any issue. In fact, you are the only one who can change your thoughts. When your thoughts are generous towards yourself and others, you will find that others are generous to you. When your thoughts tell you that others are always going to be rude to you or treat you badly, you will always interpret your experiences through this filter, and hence you'll find that the world treats you badly.

During a full two hours of phone calls, I discovered that most care providers only catered to their own clients for any type of day outings. We were with Blue Care, and they did not seem to have a social out and about program at all. Many places, including Blue Care, offered day respite at a centre. At the various centres, care was provided, as well as activities, games, music, and more. Lunch and morning tea were provided.

I knew better than to organise something like that for Geoffrey at that time, as he did not like games, and there was no way in the world he would participate in their activities. He was brought up on a farm, and the only activity was doing farm work. Games were frivolous! On some rainy days with the Alzheimer's Out and About Program, they would go to their centre in Mudgeeraba. Geoffrey always complained bitterly on those days that it was boring.

Some care providers offered shopping trips, but that was not what we were looking for. Geoffrey enjoyed going to different places, seeing the sights, enjoying the views, and having some social aspect to the day. After about twelve phone calls, I had a possible program for him—but only a maybe. It was a Friday, and I had to wait for someone to call me back the following week.

The next Thursday came, and Geoffrey went off to his last trip with Alzheimer's Australia. I expected him to come home happy that he'd had a great day. The reality was very different. As it turned out, the boss did *not* tell his staff anything. Geoffrey mentioned that it was his last trip with them just as they were dropping him home after the outing. The lovely care workers knew nothing about this and were shocked and a bit upset.

When Geoffrey told me what had happened, I was furious and very disappointed for him. I would usually call myself a make-it-happen person, but it was too late to phone them, so I waited until the next day and I phoned the office. The boss was away for a number of days, so I spoke to the next in charge, with whom I'd had good interactions in the past.

I explained the situation, what the boss had told me, and the reality of what had occurred. I expressed concern not just for Geoffrey but for the staff, who had known nothing of the boss's decision. She said she would look into it and phone me on Monday.

On Monday morning, she called me back. She had looked into everything, checked the records, and spoken to the staff. I still had not been able to find a suitable replacement outing for Geoffrey, and it was suggested that he attend for two more weeks, which would give me time to organise something else *and* give the staff some time to organise a proper goodbye for Geoffrey.

When the real last day came around, Geoffrey was given a right royal send-off, and everyone made a fuss of him. Chloe, one of the beautiful care workers, gave us a magnificent black-and-white enlarged and framed photo of Geoffrey which she had taken. It was truly a perfect picture of Geoffrey, and we both loved it. I was both very relieved and very pleased at how well his last outing with them had turned out.

13

At the start of June, Geoffrey had a fall. Early one morning, he decided to get up to adjust the blanket on the bed. He lost his balance and fell over. The first I knew of it was when he was calling me to help him get up. He was OK, thank goodness.

By now, Geoffrey was using the Luggie fairly well. He still became cross when I directed him in any way. Unfortunately, his awareness was not always that good, and he almost ran into people many times, or he'd back over them or knocks into things. I was not allowed to direct him at all. On the whole, he seemed to get better at managing it, and we bumbled through shopping centres or supermarkets somewhat carefully.

One bad experience came when we went out to the hardware store, Bunnings. Geoffrey forgot to let go the toggle, and he banged into the wall of the lift. The battery jumped out of its slot. I attempted to push it back into place while Geoffrey was trying to push me out of the way and growling at me that, "I'm OK, I can manage it!" He was actually unable to reach the battery under the seat, so I had to do it, but he was making it physically very difficult.

Eventually, I pushed the battery back into place. By this time, we had reached the first floor, and the doors had opened and closed again. Because Geoffrey was then flustered, it took quite a time for him to do a three- or four- or five-point turn in order to exit the lift. All the while, he continued to criticise me.

As we moved through the store, I suggested that Geoffrey turn the speed dial and slow down a little. He cursed at me. I found what

I needed, and when Geoffrey was about to run into a display stand again, I suggested that he slow down. He cursed at me again and told me to shut up.

My blood boiled. I was doing my best to keep him (and others) safe, and all I got was a bad attitude. I reacted to him and retorted, "I'll damn well shut up. I've had enough of even talking to you!" I turned and headed for the checkout.

I could see that Geoffrey was headed the wrong way and was not in a position to turn around right there. Nevertheless, I kept going. I passed a staff member, and he enquired kindly as to how I was today. I replied sharply, "I'm fine, but I don't know about the prick on the scooter behind me!" At the checkout, I asked if they traded in husbands. The sweet lady said it wasn't the first time she'd been asked that.

I did not speak to him at all. I was angry and hurt. We got back to the car in silence. I folded up the Luggie and put it into the boot, drove us home, took the Luggie out, and plugged it into the power so that it would recharge, all in silence. Geoffrey had been extra difficult lately, and this was the last straw. I needed some proper time off. I needed it soon.

I sat in the office and just cried. I had to let it all out. I felt as if everything and everyone mattered more than I did. The balance of our relationship was severely out of kilter. I felt as though I could not have a moment of peace until everything, every single thing, was sorted first with Geoffrey. It was most disheartening, exhausting, and heavy. Deep breathing, a drink of water, and a face wash enabled me to take action.

I made some phone calls, eventually getting on to the Commonwealth Emergency Respite people. It was a Wednesday, and they were able to give me forty-eight hours off that next weekend. Oh my God, I was so grateful. I was really at the end of my rope! They provided in-home carers for Geoffrey, and I took off to the Sunshine Coast.

Saturday, I did some shopping for myself, then I drove up to Caloundra and enjoyed the beachfront, the cafes, and the sunshine. Breathing in the fresh sea air, I could feel the tension leave my body. I felt free. I spent the rest of the weekend with my daughter Fiona, and we had a lovely time just hanging out together. When I returned home first thing Monday morning, I felt refreshed and much, much better.

———◆———

The next week, we had a house full of people from Melbourne. Family and very close friends came to stay. It was somewhat chaotic, although at the same time, everything flowed well with nine adults, one toddler, and an extra dog in the house. I had spent the previous week or so coaching Geoffrey to have his naps on the bed in the bedroom rather than try to nap in the chair, as he had been doing, while the house was full of people. Thankfully, he did do this, and he took himself off regularly to nap away from the noise and bustle. It was obvious to everyone that Geoffrey had declined physically and cognitively.

Tamara and her lovely dog stayed on longer. The three of us went out to a golf club for lunch. It had a lovely view and good food. We each ordered our meals, and we ordered a serving of vegetables to share. Geoffrey, oblivious to anything, not only started to eat his meal with his fingers but also helped himself to the vegetables with his fingers.

Tamara quietly asked him if he could please use the fork. He looked surprised, and I explained that the vegetables were for the three of us to share. He did use his fork, but shortly after proceeded to pile *all* the vegetables onto his own plate. I stopped him and said, "You've had plenty. Tamara hasn't had any yet; maybe leave the rest for her."

He frowned at me and grumped, "OK then."

Tamara and I just exchanged a look. I knew she understood.

Fiona and the children came down from the Sunshine Coast the following Thursday night to stay until Sunday night. Geoffrey was looking very pale and seemed to have very little energy for anything. It wasn't really much of a surprise when on Friday night or the early hours of Saturday morning, Geoffrey woke me saying that he couldn't breathe very well, and so we called the ambulance. Geoffrey was admitted to hospital and then treated with high-dose antibiotics, as tests showed he had a very bad UTI yet again. That's why he had not looked so good lately and probably why he was sleeping a lot more than usual.

The universe works in amazing ways. I had been wondering how I was going to get to a talk on "Pain and Consciousness" that Saturday afternoon which I wanted to attend, as I knew I was not going to be able to leave Geoffrey by himself if the girls had wanted to take the children out on Saturday. I had been sure when I replied to the beautiful Mitch Hunter that I would be there for his first public talk, but I'd had no idea how I was going to manage this. The venue was up a flight of stairs, and Geoffrey, even if he had been well enough, was not going to be able to get into the venue.

I had been mentoring Mitch for a long time, and it was exciting that he had finally put together a presentation that was both physiologically sound as well as holistically and spiritually grounded. It turned out that Geoffrey was being very well cared for in hospital, and I was free to attend the talk.

On Sunday, Geoffrey was discharged with some antibiotics. We drove Tamara and her dog to the airport on the Monday late morning so they could return to Melbourne. On the way home from the airport, Geoffrey asked me what the doctor from the hospital had said about the kit. I had no idea what he was talking about, so I asked him what he meant.

He stammered, "What the doctor said about the ah … ah … ah … ah … ah … you know, the ah … ah … ah … the ah … the kit … the asthma kit."

I told myself not to react, as Geoffrey was most adamant that he knew what he was talking about and no amount of me explaining to him that not only was there no such thing as an asthma kit but also that he didn't have asthma. He was unable to grasp the fact that his wheezing and inability to breathe sometimes was due to heart failure not asthma.

He got very aggressive about what he *knew* the doctor said, and he became very angry with me because I didn't intend to go to the chemist to get one for him. I guess he must have dreamed it up, but I knew that if I agreed with him on this and said I'd get one and brush it off, he would nag me and complain every day until I got this something called an asthma kit for him. There were certain things he would forget, but stuff like this, he'd remember.

So we were on our own after dropping Tamara at the airport, and I was in the doghouse with him within minutes. Not a great feeling, I can tell you. Inside, I screamed to myself, "Come back, everyone! I can't do this on my own!" But it was only on the inside, and nothing changed.

———◆———

INSIGHT – NINE

Accepting that everything is as it is meant to be saves us an enormous amount of stress. Often, because we are unable to understand the big picture, it can be hard to accept the is-ness of things. When we push the river or fight the flow, we are only making things harder for ourselves. When we remember to let it flow, we are allowing God/the universe/our souls to support us and assist in creating what is meant to be. Although this sounds simplistic, you will find that when you let go, release control, throw your hands in the air, or just give up trying to sort or fix things, issues will have a way of working themselves out.

I will note here that you don't have to put up with abuse or violence and just accept it as is, because in situations like that, there will be other lessons for you. Most often, the lesson will be to value yourself enough to pick yourself up by the bootstraps and walk away, get help, or move to a safe environment. This offers opportunities to boost your self-confidence and take action. The lesson may be to stand up for yourself, to empower yourself, and to do whatever it takes to create a happy, fulfilled, and rewarding life.

As Geoffrey's cognitive function seemed to be deteriorating, I asked our home care package manager if he could arrange a reassessment. I knew I would find it too challenging to shower Geoffrey, as I'd been unable to kneel or squat since I had both knees replaced in 2011. The reassessment was promptly scheduled for the following week but had to be postponed because Geoffrey was admitted to hospital for a couple of days when he had fluid on the lungs again and—guess what?—another

UTI. He was kept in for two days, given intravenous antibiotics, and then sent home with some very strong oral antibiotics.

Geoffrey started his new outings with Liberty Community Connect on 20 June. It was a slighter shorter day out. His previous bus trips collected him around 8.30 a.m., and he was home sometime between 2.30 and 3 p.m. With Liberty, it was a 9 a.m. collection and a 2 p.m. drop-off home. Just a little more restricting for me, but it covered the time I was working at the cafe well. He did not warm to the new outing immediately. I knew it would take some time for him to get used to the different people and a different outing routine.

During the next visit to our GP, we found out that the ultrasound Geoffrey had had a while back showed that he was not fully emptying his bladder. That gave us the probable cause of his UTIs. He was still asking about his asthma kit, and when he asked the doctor, she looked puzzled. I explained that it was something Geoffrey thought one of the hospital doctors had mentioned. Our lovely GP explained to Geoffrey that he didn't have asthma. Finally, he listened, and he stopped nagging me to get that special kit.

14

I n early July, Geoffrey was reassessed by an ACAT assessor. After a full and comprehensive interview, the assessor said she would recommend that Geoffrey be approved for a level 4 package but that it might take some time for him to receive one. He'd be put on the wait-list for this. It could take three months, or it could take a year or more. She had no control over that.

A cardiologist visit was next, and Geoffrey's heart medication was increased slightly. The following week, he complained of chest pain throughout the day. He had a spray of GTN under his tongue, but although the pain eased each time, it did not fully resolve.

At around 5 p.m. on Thursday, 5 July, we called the ambulance. Although it was only thirteen days since he'd finished the strong dose of antibiotics, he had another UTI. This was *so* frustrating. However, this time they did admit him and transferred him to the acute care for elderly ward. The medical team looking after him there seemed to me to be more thorough and wanted to check a few more things than had been done previously.

I spent the majority of each day in the hospital with him, because when he was in his dementia brain, he would give the doctors and nurses inaccurate answers, and I didn't want him overmedicated, which was what had happened when they were given information by the patient that indicated a different problem or symptoms to the actuality.

Geoffrey was with it on and off throughout the first couple of days, and then he came good and was much more like his usual self. He was having quite vivid dreams, though, and he would wake after a bit of a doze and start making comments or have questions about things that did not make sense. Usually, I could laugh and say to him, "I think maybe my brain isn't working today, because I have no idea what you are talking about." When he found that he couldn't actually remember what he was on about, I'd suggest it might have been a dream, and he would usually be OK about it and go back to sleep.

Occasionally he would want to argue, and then I'd just agree with whatever it was until he was happy to go back to sleep. Next time he woke up, he'd have no recollection of our conversation. It was quite comical and made me giggle. I felt a little guilty at having a laugh at his expense, but it really was funny.

———◆———

I put a couple of posts on Facebook to let everyone know how Geffrey was doing and that he was spending several days in hospital. I was blown away by how many messages of support I received. Many people sent their love, prayers, and healing energy. Many offered a short message to say they were thinking of us. Others sent private messages or texts. I had so many people who knew us both—some of whom I hadn't had a great deal of contact with for a while and a large number of others who only knew me personally and not Geoffrey—send wonderful messages with heartfelt wishes. It was staggering.

I had phone calls from people wanting to know if I needed any support. Was there anything they could do for me? When I shared the messages with Geoffrey, it put a lovely big smile on his face. He said that he felt loved.

It truly warmed my heart to know that we were cared for. I knew that I had many people I could call for help if and when I needed it. I knew that Geoffrey was ill, but my heart was full.

We were told at 9.45 a.m. on the morning of the Tuesday that he could go home. He'd been in hospital five days this time. He appeared to be stable except for poor bladder control. He was packed up and ready to go within ten minutes. Over an hour later, the pharmacist finally came and gave me his medication list and a prescription for the new antibiotic he'd been put on. The nurse said that the doctor had ordered an iron infusion for Geoffrey before he was discharged. So we waited.

The nurse came in at 11.30 a.m. and said that it shouldn't be much longer, she was just waiting for the RN. Then it was lunchtime. Geoffrey had his lunch. I went down to the hospital cafe and then brought the food for myself up to the ward. We ate and we waited some more.

I remembered that I'd parked in a three-hour zone and it was just a little over the three hours, so I went down to the car park to move my car. Too late—I had a parking ticket! There went $150! I moved the car anyway, returned to the ward, and waited. My patience was being tested. I was not impressed at, one, waiting so long when we'd been told that Geoffrey could go home this morning, and two, getting that stupid ticket.

Geoffrey was becoming antsy. He wanted to go home, as it had been hours since he'd been told that he could go. I went to the nurses' station and enquired as to how much longer it might be. It was 1.30 p.m. The RN who was to do the iron infusion casually said she'd do it after lunch, then corrected herself and said she'd do it after the shift change at 2.30 p.m., and that it would take about an hour.

I said that it was after lunch already, and I was waiting to take Geoffrey home. I had to be home by 3.45 p.m., as I had someone coming and I had to be there.

"Oh, OK," she said reluctantly. "I'll do it now."

We waited, but she did not come to do the infusion. When it was almost 2 p.m., Geoffrey was transferred to the transit lounge, and we were told that they would do the infusion there. They needed his bed in the ward for someone else.

I moved the car around to the other side of the hospital where the transit section was and I found that all the parking available was fifteen minutes only. I parked and went inside. I was then told that the infusion would take two hours. Two hours! Not impressed!

I was stressed. My tears escaped; I could not keep them in. This felt really hard, and it had been a long day. There was nothing anyone could do about the situation. I did not want another parking ticket, so reluctantly, I left Geoffrey there and told them I'd collect him at 5.30 p.m., which was when I thought I'd be free to go back.

I cried all the way home. I had to let it out. I wasn't feeling sorry for myself; I was just feeling overwhelmed and frustrated. What a waste of a day! I felt as though nothing had been achieved that day, and money had been wasted too. I had to do some serious talking to myself to maintain any sort of balance, and deep breaths saved my sanity.

Geoffrey, although he said he felt better after the iron infusion, was exhausted by the time I got him home at 5.30 p.m. Hearty vegetable soup, which I'd made the day before, was dinner, and Geoffrey was well and truly ready for bed before 8.30 p.m.

———◆◆◆———

Geoffrey woke me at around midnight. At first, I thought, *Oh no, he can't breathe again. We'll need an ambulance.* Then I realised he was talking and breathing normally, so I moved on to, Oh *goodness, he's having heart pains. I'll need to call an ambulance!* In the next instant, I pulled myself from sleep and asked what the matter was. He said that he had wet the bed. He was miserable and confused about it, saying that he didn't have any idea how that had happened. He was wearing a pull-up pad. Nevertheless, the evidence was there: a wet bed.

I jumped up, pulled the sheets off the bed, and grabbed some towels to dry up the wet patch. Geoffrey wanted to help me, but his lack of good balance and the slow pace of his movements meant that it was far easier for him to just sit in the chair. I remade the bed with fresh sheets, using towels over the wet patch and under the mattress protector. All the while I reassured him that *it's OK, not a problem, stuff happens, it's easily fixed,* and so on. I knew that he felt awful at having done it with no recollection.

We climbed back into bed, and I told him again to not stress over it. "It's called an accident, not an "on purpose"! We'll look into getting better-fitting pull-ups for night-time." He apologised for waking me and giving me more work. I told him not to worry about it and reassured him that *it's all fixed for now, it's not a problem, I'm fine, I'm here to help and support you, and it's OK.* I said, "Sleep well. Wake me if you need anything else." We both slept well for the rest of the night.

The next day, I phoned Geoffrey's package manager and asked that Geoffrey move up the list for the continence nurse appointment. Instead of that, in the afternoon, the manager kindly brought several samples of different pull-ups for us to try. Then we only had to phone him to get them ordered. He ordered some bed protection as well, which he said would take a couple of days to arrive.

Because it was only his first day out of hospital, Geoffrey didn't feel up to going on the bus trip. I cancelled that early in the morning, and I took him over to Lyn and Paul's place so that I could go to see a couple of clients who were booked in to see me at the cafe. Once I collected him, he wanted to get out, and we went to a local cafe for a light lunch.

On the way home, he suddenly looked very tired. Geoffrey went to bed and had a sleep as soon as we got home. When he awoke, he informed me that he'd had chest pain all day. When he described what was going on, it sounded more like indigestion. I gave him something for that, and he went back to sleep.

Once he was up from his sleep, he said that his chest pain was worse and that it was very sharp when he breathed in deeply. The pain was strong. Even after a couple of sprays of GTN, the pain was still quite severe. So it came to pass that only twenty-four hours after he was discharged from hospital, he was in an ambulance headed back there. One of the beautiful ambulance officers suggested that Geoffrey was just trying to rack up frequent-flyer points from the ambulance service. I had to laugh, but in reality, I was frustrated.

As I was driving to the hospital to meet the ambulance, I quickly phoned Tamara. I told her what was happening, and I wailed in a mock-whine voice, "I don't want to do this again! It's not fair. I can't keep doing this. Boohoo, boohoo." It did work to relieve some of my frustration, as we laughed at my little-girl whine voice. It actually felt really good to get it out.

I didn't leave the hospital until after eleven that night. I was tired. It took me a fair while before I could sleep. Geoffrey was only kept in overnight, and I had him home again by mid-morning. He was still somewhat breathless, and he had a cough.

Although it didn't sound like extra work when Geoffrey was in hospital, with all of his recent admissions, there were extra things which were tiresome. I called Liberty to let them know that as Geoffrey had just come out of hospital on Tuesday evening, he wasn't up to a bus trip on Wednesday. Then I called our friend Paul to see if I could leave Geoffrey with him for a while on Wednesday morning so that I could go to the cafe and see clients. Paul could only help out until eleven, because he had to take Lyn to a specialist for something, so then I had to tell the cafe that I couldn't stay all morning as usual, so they had to reschedule some people until the next week. I called Blue Care to cancel the care worker for Thursday when Geoffrey was readmitted. I called my art teacher to tell her I couldn't be at class that day. Then I called Blue Care again, as the only GP appointment I could get was Friday morning, and so the Friday home respite service had to be cancelled too.

It was difficult not to feel as though my world was turned upside down, but I plodded through all the calls and did my best not to take over-responsibility for the extra clients who wanted to see me on Wednesday or for making a nuisance of myself with so many calls to Blue Care.

Geoffrey's urinary incontinence worsened. I was glad when the Kylies bed protection arrived. Geoffrey tried on a couple of the pull-up samples we had. We found which ones fitted the best and placed an order through Blue Care. Yes, another call to Blue Care! Thank you, Lesley, for your care and understanding.

———◆———

INSIGHT – TEN

We are all only responsible for ourselves. Caring and compassion are important qualities in balance. These qualities are out of balance when we find that we are continually trying to fix the world, fix other people's problems, or be the one to come to the rescue. This does not mean that we don't have compassion for others; it means that we stay responsible for ourselves and help to empower others to take responsibility for themselves also.

When we rush in to rescue others, there is often an underlying need for us to be approved of—or we get to feel good about ourselves because we are seen to be helping others. In reality, we can assist others in a more balanced and empowering way when we love and approve of ourselves, and our inner motives are purely loving and caring.

It is easy, when we are naturally caring and giving, to take an excess amount of responsibility for others. You can recognise this when you are making decisions for someone without asking permission or you are pushing for others to have more than they are allowing for themselves. This is an easy trap to fall into when you truly care about someone.

Balanced, loving actions require you to check in with people as to what they desire rather than acting upon what you desire for them or what you think they need. It is balanced and loving to allow others to make their own decisions and to experience the positive or negative consequences of their choices, while you continue to love them the same anyway.

15

A visit to our GP gave her the picture of what was going on. At the hospital, they had made it quite clear that there was nothing they could do except try to keep Geoffrey's symptoms under control. The hospital doctors had said to expect him to have a major heart attack one day from which he would not recover. It might be soon, or it might be a long time away. They had no idea.

Our lovely GP was concerned as to how I was with that. I was able to say that really, I was relatively prepared, inasmuch as anyone can be prepared for such a thing. She was very caring, reassuring me that I was to see her for anything that she could help with. She was there for me.

As far as the apartment went, it looked like it was still going to be almost two years until it was ready, as the dig had not even begun and it was mid-July. I was talking to an acquaintance about how Geoffrey was, and she told me that she would have a granny flat ready at her place by about the end of the year. It sounds callous, but I needed to keep my plans flowing. The fact that there might be a place for me to go that would work out cheaper and easier than staying in the house by myself should Geoffrey die gave me peace of mind. I could get the things done around the house which needed attention, sell the house, and take myself and my dogs to the granny flat until my apartment was built. It did give me some peace of mind, as I knew I could not afford to stay in this big house, nor could I manage it and the garden ongoing by myself.

I found that I seriously needed to get to the supermarket. I also needed to buy Geoffrey some tracksuit pants. He had lost some weight, and his jeans were not only too big, they were a problem for him to undo when he had to go to the toilet.

We went to Kmart, and I found some trackpants for him and also a medium-weight long-sleeved washable top. Keeping him in clean clothes was a job in itself. Over the last few years, he had soiled his tops and jumpers at a great rate. Every meal or snack, he would make a mess. He would drop food on himself, spill drinks, and so forth. Three of his lightweight jumpers had holes in the front of them. I had no idea how he did this. This was becoming worse, and his woollen jumpers were not exactly easy wash-and-wear material.

Geoffrey was using the Luggie, and when we were shopping, he was not able to take his jumper off by himself in order to try on our selection of tops. He became confused as to why he needed to take his jumper off, and as I was trying to help him out of the jumper he was wearing, he started fighting me and trying to get his jumper back on.

I stopped and reminded him of what we were doing, and then he complied. I helped him out of it and then helped him on with one top which proved to be too small. I helped him off with that. I turned my back to grab the next size up, and he had already started to put on his old jumper—back to front, I might add.

I explained again that I needed him to try the next size. I helped get his arms out of his jumper again and helped him get the larger size one on. It fit! OK, now I had to help him take it off so I could take it to the checkout and pay for it. I helped him to put on his old jumper for the last time. I didn't know about him, but I was exhausted!

We stopped at a cafe to have some lunch. Geoffrey decided that he wanted pancakes and coffee. If that was his choice, then that's what I would order for him. He was still in the Luggie, but he forgot to slow the speed down as we entered the cafe. He rounded a corner way too fast, and although a customer kindly moved her chair so that Geoffrey could get through, he flew past me and crashed into the side of the customers' table. Thank goodness they had finished their coffee, or they'd have been wearing it!

I grabbed at the handlebar of the Luggie and tried to get Geoffrey to release the accelerator. But he was clinging tight. I quickly prised his finger off the toggle and turned the dial to slow, and he came to a stop. At the same time, he growled at me that he was OK.

I apologised to the ladies and helped them move their table back into place. Geoffrey was totally unaware of what he had done. I was acutely aware of people's stares and disapproval. I apologised again and I moved another chair out of the way so that Geoffrey could pull up next to an empty table.

Geoffrey's method of eating had declined. He seemed to be using his fingers first rather than any cutlery more and more often now. When our pancakes came, he spread the ice cream onto one, folded it in half, and started to stuff it into his mouth. Of course, the ice cream melted and ran onto his plate, his jumper, and down the front edge of the table, I snatched up the serviette and quickly wiped his jumper and the edge of the table, then proceeded to eat my meal. There was no point in asking him to use the cutlery provided, so I just kept an eye out for the drips and continued to enjoy my lunch.

I was aware of the looks from other people as Geoffrey stuffed in large mouthfuls at a time. He had butter and ice cream all over his hands and face and didn't seem to care. I had noticed that at home, he had been doing the same thing, often putting very large amounts at a time onto his spoon or fork or using his fingers. I had been reminding him for a long time now to wipe his face, as he often made a mess and didn't notice when his face or his hands were covered in food. Often, I would just get a wet cloth and wipe his hands and face myself when he was finished. As we were out on this occasion, I got up from my seat, went to the counter, took some more serviettes, and simply wiped him up.

<hr />

Geoffrey wanted to go to the farmers market with me on Sunday. Although he did not have a shower, it took a while to get out the door, as he now needed help to get dressed. This meant I helped with getting his pull-ups on, his trousers or trackpants on, his jumper on, and his sock and shoes on. I also put drops into his eyes every morning and moisturising cream on his legs and feet, as they were very dry. All this was a very slow process. While I went to get all his supplements and medications out, I told him to have a shave. He didn't. Instead, he went and waited in the car. So I packed my market trolley and his Luggie into the car, and off we went.

It was a glorious sunny morning, although still a little chilly at 7.30 a.m. Once we arrived at the market, I put the shopping trolley together and took the Luggie out of the car and got it ready for Geoffrey to use. We had an enjoyable time shopping, buying our beautiful fresh fruit, veggies, and a couple of yummy treats. We ate breakfast in the sunshine, listened to the buskers' music, had our coffee, and soaked in the atmosphere. I loved it.

By the time we were ready to leave, however, the market was bustling with people. Rather than Geoffrey trying to make his way through all the people at the various stalls, we headed around the playground and into the car park. Carefully going through, we moved past parked cars and then entered the car park where our car was.

Geoffrey wandered into the middle of the road. I asked him to keep to the edge because it was a road and people in cars looking for places to park were cruising around. He crabbily retorted that there was nothing coming. I insisted that he move closer to the edge because he was in the middle of the road and it wasn't safe.

"OK, bossy boots!" he snapped. Then he moved a little closer to me. Only a *little* closer, though.

When we arrived at our parked car, Geoffrey managed to head straight for me. I was at the boot of the car, and I was waiting for him to pull up and turn the Luggie to park next to his passenger-side door like usual. Instead, he was going too fast, and he ploughed into me and the back corner of the car. Fortunately, I had seen it coming, and I lurched forward to pull his hand off the accelerator. Of course, he was gripping it tightly, and as he crashed into me and the back corner of the car, I only just managed to pry his hand loose and stop the Luggie. I knew that I would have a bruise or two, but no damage was done to the car.

Naturally, I was yelling at him at the top of my lungs by the time he came to a stop. It was a good outlet of frustration for me, but it only increased his bad humour. We did a physical battle over the controls of the Luggie so that the Luggie reversed and then moved forward alongside the car. Geoffrey was cursing me the whole time. He thought that it was OK because the car wasn't damaged.

I was furious. "It's not f***ing OK!" I screamed. "You are dangerous. If you're not going to listen to me, I won't ever take the Luggie with us again. I'll sell the damn thing if you are not going to use it safely!" My raised voice caused a number of people at the market stalls in front of the car to stop and stare at us. I ignored them.

I stopped the Luggie as we got to Geoffrey's door. I opened the door and helped him off. Then I drove the Luggie to the back of the car so that I could put it into the boot. All was quiet. Geoffrey did not say a word all the way home. I felt a bit mean, but I knew that when he acted like a child, I needed to treat him like a child. I felt as if it was the only way I could get some messages through to him.

Later, I thought that what probably happened was that he cruised along at a regular speed, then when he needed to navigate smaller spaces, he forgot to turn down the speed. In a small space, when the Luggie's speed wasn't turned down, it lurched forwards, and Geoffrey, rather than letting the toggle go, which was what he needed to do, squeezed it tighter in panic, creating havoc. With the last two incidents, I had not reminded him to turn down the speed. Needless to say, in the past, when I reminded him to turn down the speed as we got to tight corners or things he needed to navigate around, he had always grumped at me, "I know. I'm OK. Stop telling me what to do!"

I acknowledged to myself that this was another rock-and-a-hard-place situation and that I'd just have to keep reminding him to slow down and then put up with the inevitable abuse and grumpiness from him.

INSIGHT – ELEVEN

What other people think is not my business. People are always going to think things. In other people's minds, we are likely to be criticised for our hair, our clothes, our weight, our colour sense, or our lack of fashion. We are judged for what we say, what we don't say, our parenting style, what we do or don't do, how we walk, the decisions we make, and much more. The question is, are you going to limit who you are and what you do or don't do based upon what other people *might* think? You are never going to know what everyone thinks, and neither do you need to know. Do you need to make other people's thoughts matter in *your* life?

It is impossible to be yourself and be true to yourself when you are busy worrying about what people think. Consider how much energy you are wasting with worry. Think about how much more freedom you could feel if you never worried about what other people thought. How much more energy would you have to use in positive pursuits?

Geoffrey's box of pull-ups arrived, but there was a problem. The company that made them had changed some things since they made the ones that our package manager gave us to try. Geoffrey could use them, but they were a little big for him. I sighed at the prospect of yet another call to Blue Care.

The next time we had a care worker, I bought a men's urine bottle for Geoffrey to use at the bedside to save him leaking before he got to the toilet at night. I also ordered some adult washable bibs online because they would be easier to wash than his jumpers.

I thought to myself, *This is getting serious!* He was making almost as much mess as a child. He couldn't make good decisions just like a child, and yet he was big and strong. He could fight me if I tried to move his hand off something, which was not like a child at all. I knew that a child was easier in many ways. I did know that, as I have certainly had plenty—three of my own children and fifteen foster children. Plus I had owned and run a childcare centre. This certainly gave me enough qualifications to know.

How did I feel about all this? How did I feel in general? I sighed deeply as I thought about it, because in many ways, I was coping all right.

I was coping with his confusion. I was coping with his incontinence. I was coping with his need for physical assistance. I was coping with his need to know where I was and what I was doing every minute of the day. I was coping with his deafness. I was coping with the constant nature of his needs. Yes, I was coping all right.

But how did I feel on the inside? I found it was very hard to pinpoint just what the feeling was. In many ways, I did feel loved and supported. I knew I could pick any number of people to phone if and when I needed to chat, or to just vent to get any frustration off my chest. I did use this option from time to time. Yet when I truly checked in with myself, I think I felt an emptiness and loneliness. A hollow feeling was sitting inside me. I felt as if somehow, I had a need that was unfillable by anyone else. My busyness kept me from sitting in, or wallowing in, that feeling, and it did not arise often.

On this day, I fell into that emptiness. In that emptiness there was sadness, somehow mixed with a knowing that I was always looked after. There was a feeling of being let down, but by whom? How? Right now, in this minute, I was OK, but the feeling persisted.

I got it! I felt let down by Geoffrey. I'd lost my bestie except when he surfaced every now and again and we would have a laugh. It didn't last long, though. I was sad. I'd been let down. It was partially grief, I guess. That was the emptiness, I think.

I knew that only I could fill that hole inside of me—no one else. I knew I had many people who loved me, so if there was a hollow feeling inside me, it could only be me who could fill it. I reminded myself to get back to using my acknowledgement journal daily. I could have done with some inner loving, some more feeling good about myself and allowing some of that to filter through to the inside of me.

INSIGHT – TWELVE

An acknowledgment journal is more than just a gratitude journal. An acknowledgement journal is used to write whatever one can acknowledge about oneself, big or small. This includes skills and abilities, actions or non-actions, feelings, steps toward a goal, or achievements. Anything positive about your day, your week, you, or your life goes into that journal. Every so often, you can go back and read your previous acknowledgements, and most often you will find that you are able to acknowledge more and more the longer you use it. You are giving yourself positive evidence which your inner critic can see and cannot dispute. That is love.

In our society, we have been taught or encouraged not to think highly of ourselves. This is one of the causes of lack of self-esteem and lack of self-love. An acknowledgement journal can correct this type of thinking. It can, when used regularly, bring us to the realisation that we are valuable just as we are and that our contributions to the world, be they big or small, have value. It is a great way of getting back in touch with our whole selves. Without any judgements, we are able to see, feel, and know our intrinsic value.

An acknowledgement journal is not for recording judgements about ourselves or others. Judgements take us out of the now moment, and when you are recording things in your journal, your aim is to feel peaceful and in a loving space of acknowledging right now. Gratitude goes hand in hand with this; however, an acknowledgment journal goes beyond gratitude. I call it gratitude plus!

16

Exactly a week after Geoffrey was discharged from hospital, he was admitted again. At 1 a.m., he woke me because he was having difficulty breathing. This time, his heart failure was exacerbated by a lung infection. Pneumonia, they said. He looked very flushed and had a high temperature. After thirty-six hours, more antibiotics, and more diuretics, his temperature was down to normal, but he was still on a small amount of oxygen. Slowly he seemed to improve.

An ultrasound showed that the mitral valve of Geoffrey's heart now had a substantial leak (regurgitation) and was causing what might be termed *back-pressure*. This in turn was causing a constant fluid build-up on the lungs as the heart struggled to keep working with so much extra back-pressure. He slowly improved.

This time, his hospital stay was seven days. When he was very sick, I could hardly notice his dementia, but he was hardly speaking, so that made a difference. On about the fifth day of his stay, he started asking questions about things that I had sorted. For example, he wanted to remind me to cancel his bus trip; I'd already done that. He asked about how his care workers would know not to come; I'd taken care of that. He asked about when the OT was coming; I'd put her on hold for the time being. It was clear that he was worrying about lots of things, because he asked me these questions and others like them several times each.

On the day before he was hopefully going to be discharged, I told Geoffrey that I couldn't get to the hospital until lunchtime the next day. He then proceeded to ask me quite a number of times what time in the morning I would come to the hospital.

I found that overall, I managed fairly well with having Geoffrey in the hospital. I did not stress, and I took things a day at a time—sometimes hour by hour as I dealt with what needed to be done. There were, of course, many phone calls to make to sort things again—cancelling the OT and Geoffrey's bus trip, putting a hold on his regular care workers, organising the extra help that Geoffrey would need when he came home (he needed more help with showering and dressing than I thought I could manage), arranging for the dog groomer to have access to the dogs from inside the house when I wasn't going to be there. There were still bills to pay, which I had to remember to do, and a couple of other commitments that I had, some of which I had to cancel for that week. Combining these things with making sure I was at the hospital as much as possible so that I could be there when the doctors came made each day fairly full.

I had long ago realised that Geoffrey could not always be relied upon to give the doctors accurate information when they asked their barrage of questions. On one occasion, I arrived just as Geoffrey told them he had some problem or other which wasn't true, and the doctor was about to prescribe a medication for it. Once I clarified the actual situation, the doctor understood that Geoffrey had been confused and had mixed up something from the present with something from sixty years ago. It was frustrating that they did not seem to read the notes to see that Geoffrey did have a level of dementia.

After seven days, I was very weary, and I had not had a good sleep the night before. Geoffrey's watch had gone missing. He remembered having it the morning before and taking it off to shower. He thought the nurse had popped it into her pocket, but he wasn't sure. I'd searched everywhere, every drawer, every pocket, every corner of the room and the bathroom.

Throughout the day, Geoffrey kept checking the drawers over and over. By late afternoon, he reached into a drawer again, and I said that we'd checked that drawer and his watch was not there. Apparently, he was only reaching for his hanky, and he snapped harshly at me, "You don't need to control everything!"

I was tired, and I allowed his nastiness to get under my skin. I felt hurt. I felt unappreciated, and it evoked a level of anger. When I snapped back at him, he had no idea what he had said to upset me. When I told him what he'd said and how I felt, he denied saying it at first, and then he said that he had no idea he'd said that. He apologised—a rare thing indeed.

By this time, I was crying and found it difficult to stop the flow of tears. Geoffrey was horrified that he had upset me so. I stayed a while, and then I gave him a big hug and a kiss as I left to go home and feed the dogs before it was late.

Geoffrey was going to be discharged as soon as it could be arranged for him to have oxygen at home. Once again, the staff had read Geoffrey's notes well, and the process was started, with lots of paperwork to be completed. When I arrived at the hospital that day, I discovered that Geoffrey had signed the papers for the oxygen, although he had no idea what he had signed. When I asked what was going on, the doctor and the specialist respiratory nurse told me about the process for getting oxygen at home.

Then they noticed that Geoffrey was on a home care package and that we were with Blue Care. This changed everything. It meant that all the paperwork was for nothing; all that was required was a letter from the doctor with all the info included that would have normally been in the usual paperwork being emailed to the home care package manager. The cost had to come out of his package money. The oxygen would be organised through Blue Care. The government would not fund it separately if a person was on a home care package, nor would they give us the usual $90 per quarter rebate on our power bill which non-home-care-package people got.

The doctor obtained the correct email address for the Blue Care package manager from me and said she'd return later and confirm that the email request had been sent. I was at the hospital until 5.30 p.m., and the doctor did not return. The next morning, I phoned the package manager myself to ensure he'd received the letter and to enquire as to how long it might be before the equipment would be delivered. I could not get a hold of him on the phone, and I had to wait for him to return my call. More waiting. I had done a lot of that in the past week!

———◆•◆◆•◆———

Throughout the week Geoffrey was in hospital, I'd received a number of text messages of love and support from family and friends. I'd received Facebook messages and phone calls too. My beautiful friends Suzy and Chris phoned me almost every day from Melbourne, and I found their calls very supportive. I spoke to them when I was feeling good and also when I was feeling overwhelmed.

As it turned out, the email to Blue Care had not been sent, and it took until late morning the next day for that to happen. I was ready to take Geoffrey home, because he was well and truly fed up and had had enough of the hospital. I had brought the Luggie into the ward so that he could drive it out to the car and we would not have to wait another hour for a wheelchair to get him to the car. Even though his medications had been changed, we did not wait for the pharmacy person to come and give me a new list and instructions. Two medications had been dropped, that's all, so I did not think it necessary to wait the hour for the pharmacist.

It felt as though we were escaping. We couldn't get out of there fast enough! Five minutes before we were about to leave, I found Geoffrey's watch hiding in a pocket of the wheelie-walker he had been using. Phew!

Geoffrey was weak, and his cognitive function was a little worse. Once at home, I made sure he stayed warm and comfortable. He needed help with almost everything. Washing, dressing, and undressing were all things he couldn't do on his own anymore. I organised with Blue Care to have help to shower and dress Geoffrey three mornings a week, which would begin the following Monday. I assisted him on the other days and helped to undress him every night. It was quite physical work, and I had to explain everything as we went along, otherwise he would fight me and would not be helpful in the process.

Geoffrey was not able to go on the bus trip on the Wednesday, and as I had no carer to stay with him, he came with me to cafe. I parked him where he could do his crossword and have a coffee. Dear Danni, the lovely cafe staff member, looked after him at the cafe, very regularly checking on him to see if he needed anything. She brought him some raisin toast and then, between clients, I helped him to a couch, and he lay back and had a snooze. It was a bit distracting having him there, and I was glad I didn't have to do that every week.

The occupational therapist had been over to assess the house, and it was determined that Geoffrey needed some things. A shower stool and 2x toilet surround/support frames eventually arrived, and they helped Geoffrey, as he was finding it hard to get up off the toilet and he was too wobbly on his feet to stand up for his shower. It was also organised to get a step for the side of the bed. A ramp at the back door would also make it easier for Geoffrey to get outside to the sunshine. Both of these things needed to be quoted on first, and so we had to wait for the quote and then wait for the items to be made.

I took Geoffrey for his regular physiotherapy appointment, The physiotherapist was appalled that the hospital physio had done nothing regarding exercises for Geoffrey's weakened legs and muscle wastage.

The oxygen converter came and was easy to use. Geoffrey used it as needed on and off throughout the daytime and occasionally at night. It did seem to give him a bit more energy, and it pinked him up. He still needed regular sleeps, rests, and naps. He was very weak in the legs. He was extremely wobbly on his feet, and his right leg appeared to be lagging a bit more than the left. He really needed to be holding on to something every step that he took. No more wobbling across the room on his own. The wheelie-walker went absolutely everywhere with him every single step.

By this time, Geoffrey was coughing a lot. It was mostly not a productive cough but a very choking type of cough. He would cough, gag, and cough some more. Sometimes it was on food, sometimes it was when he took a drink, and sometimes it was for no reason. His face would go bright red as he choked, and he would be unable to catch his breath. Sometimes a good thump on the back helped. Sometimes there was nothing to be done but give him a towel to cough and splutter into. It was scary to watch, as it sometimes looked as though he was just going to choke totally.

———————◆•◆•◆———————

I let Erin, in New Zealand, know that her dad was pretty sick and I had no idea how long we would have him for. Within the week, she and Roger came over for four days. To say that their visit was a godsend is an understatement. I felt so supported. I was able to have some good company as well as some assistance with Geoffrey.

On Erin's birthday, we had lunch at a beautiful seafood restaurant. Apart from Geoffrey almost taking the Luggie through a window, the lunch went well. Geoffrey was finding it hard to use his knife and fork, so Roger tucked Geoffrey's napkin into his shirt, and in doing so, saved Geoffrey's jumper from getting totally messed on. Happy Birthday, Erin. It was a lovely day. Geoffrey slept most of the afternoon.

Geoffrey's coughing fits became worse one afternoon, and then we realised that the windows were open and the cold air was making his cough worse. Drinking with a straw lessened the risk of him having a coughing fit but didn't totally stop them.

Geoffrey was eating badly, and he was overloading his fork or spoon and trying to stuff huge amounts into his mouth at once. Usually, this resulted in food being dropped onto the plate, the table, and down Geoffrey's front. Erin suggested that we all use smaller forks and smaller spoons so that Geoffrey couldn't get quite so much on his. This worked to a point, but only while Erin and Roger were there. As soon as they left, he grumped about the small cutlery and got up and helped himself to a regular-size spoon or fork.

I had no problem with Roger driving my car, so during their four days at our place, they were able to get out and about themselves and do some personal shopping, assist me, spend time with Geoffrey, and also do a couple of jobs in the garden which I was physically unable to manage. On the Sunday, we went to the farmers market. Geoffrey was cognitively very challenged that weekend, and despite me reminding him to go up the centre of the ramp from the road, Geoffrey took the corner hard and rode up the side of the ramp. Of course, the Luggie almost toppled over sideways. It veered off to the side, and Geoffrey slammed into the side rail because he'd gripped the accelerator tight instead of letting it go.

The three of us quickly rescued him and got him back onto the centre of the ramp. An almost disaster! The rest of the morning was good, except Geoffrey's lack of awareness meant that as I walked beside him, he crept over towards me, and he fought my assistance when I tried to turn the Luggie away from me slightly. Consequently, I ended up in the bushes. He was amazingly resistant to being guided in any way. Anyway, we enjoyed some good music and breakfast by the lake after we shopped for all our fresh fruit and vegetables.

When we got back to the car, as usual, I reminded Geoffrey to park the Luggie a little away from the car in order for him to have some space to get up from the Luggie and be able to get into the car. He fought with me over this and insisted that he was all right and knew what he was doing. I became cross, grabbed the control, and manoeuvred the Luggie away from the car with Geoffrey complaining the whole time. *Helping him shouldn't be this hard*, I thought.

I truly did not want Erin and Roger to go home at the end of the four days. Apart from when I tried to get him to the car safely, Geoffrey hadn't grumped much at me the whole time of their visit. It was lovely, and I appreciated their support in many ways. Thank you. I love you Erin.

On the Monday I was to take Erin and Roger to the airport, we had to leave by 9 a.m. I thought that would work out fine; the Blue Care worker was due, I thought, to come and give Geoffrey his shower at 8.30 a.m. and then would stay until 11 a.m. Erin and Roger could say goodbye to Geoffrey at home, and then I was free to take them to the airport. However, by ten to nine, no one had arrived. When I phoned Blue Care. I was told that the care worker wasn't scheduled to come until 9.15 that day. I was not at all impressed. I quickly helped Geoffrey get dressed, as it meant that he had to go with us to the airport, un-showered and unshaven.

I was a bit frustrated. I thought I had been clear when we organised the Monday care worker for shower and a couple of hours respite for me to get out of the house on my own that 8.30 a.m. was the latest time that would work for us. Geoffrey would, on those days, have his breakfast and was happy to do that with his dressing-gown and slippers on. With dementia, routine is everything, and Geoffrey would become anxious and stressed if he had to wait too late for a shower and shave. Yet another phone call to Blue Care was required to sort this out. It doesn't sound like much, but all these little things on top of the everyday management of Geoffrey was draining me.

By the time it came to Wednesday that week, Geoffrey was considerably better physically, although still very wobbly on his feet, so he went on the bus trip. I was a bit nervous about it, as I wasn't fully sure that he was up to it. He was exhausted when he returned home and slept for two hours straight.

17

We were invited to a function at the development where I was buying the apartment. These soirees, hosted by the developers, were held every four months or so, and we had already attended a couple. It was a lovely social gathering where we were able to meet people who were already living in the completed apartments plus the people who were buying into the same building as us.

I thought that Geoffrey probably wasn't up to it, and I suggested that I take him over to stay with Lyn and Paul for a few hours so that I could go.

"No, no," he said emphatically. "I'll come with you!"

Against my better judgement, I loaded the Luggie into the car, and off we went. When we arrived, I unfolded the Luggie and parked it at the back of the car on the passenger side. It was not a disabled car park, so the space wasn't wide enough to get the Luggie down the side of the car.

Geoffrey took a long time getting out of the car and, holding on to the side of the car, slowly making his way to the Luggie. I held on to him to stabilise him, and he finally sat down. The Luggie was already facing the way we needed to go.

With the memory of him almost toppling over at the market the previous Sunday, I reminded him to go up the middle of the pathway up the kerb.

"I know," he snapped.

As we made our way up the path and then the ramp, Geoffrey drove the Luggie sideways towards me, giving me less and less room on the path. I was looking away to the side at the time, admiring the garden. The result was that he tripped me up as I took a step by running the Luggie into my legs. Suddenly, I felt as though I was flying through the air, and I landed very hard onto the concrete rampway.

My knees and my elbow and both wrists landed hard. The worst was my ribs and left breast area. I found myself totally winded, and it was very hard to regain my breath. I lay there for a few moments, gasping like a fish, just trying to catch my breath.

The lovely lady who was at the top of the ramp waiting to open the gate for us rushed over and asked if I was OK. Did I need an ambulance? Was I OK to get up? She was very concerned. Once I got my breath and could breathe normally, I realised I was only bruised and scraped a little on my hands. I was able to get up, and as we continued in to the function, she rushed to get me an ice pack to put on my hands and wrists. During this whole time, Geoffrey said absolutely nothing.

Geoffrey did not want to stay seated on the Luggie—something which he conveyed to me in a grumpy series of grunts and gestures. I helped him to a chair at one of the tables that was the furthest from the noise and chatter, busyness, and movement of people. I parked the Luggie out of the way, and I proceeded to collect drinks for us— champagne and orange juice for me, soft drink for Geoffrey. He still said absolutely nothing.

We were joined by a few people, and I chatted with them. One was a current apartment owner and the other a prospective owner looking at buying an apartment in the block in which we had purchased. I enjoyed the company and we were well catered for with a hearty selection of delicious canapés. We were told that there was a new show apartment with the same finishes the apartments in our building would have, and we could do a tour.

One group was taken through the apartment. It was already a big group, so I was told that we could go with the next one. Then Geoffrey needed to use a toilet. Because the new sauna and gymnasium building were being built right next to the outdoor area where the function was being held, we had to proceed to the old show apartment—out of the area, back down the ramps, down the path, and into the building across from the car park.

As we approached the door, I indicated to Geoffrey to take a wide swing so that he could get through the door easily, and I reminded him to turn the speed down to slow. He did not touch the speed dial, so I reached over and turned it down myself. He did not swing anywhere near wide enough, though, and he came crashing into the door frame despite everyone's yells for him to stop before he hit it. Bang!

Thankfully, there was no paint damage to the door frame. He hit it hard, and the Luggie's battery jumped out of position, which in turn stopped it from working at all. I reached down and pushed the battery back into place. I quickly pushed the free-wheel mode lever and took control of the steering whilst pushing the Luggie backwards, with Geoffrey aboard, to create a better angle for him to reapproach the doorway. I re-engaged the lever and turned the Luggie back on.

Geoffrey managed to negotiate the turn this time, and I guided him to the toilet with the easiest access. I entered the bathroom first, and as Geoffrey entered, he lost control of the Luggie because there was a very slight rise at the entrance. The Luggie could cope with it; Geoffrey could not. He ploughed half into me and half into the vanity unit.

I'd quickly grabbed the handlebar, and while I yelled out for him to *stop! stop! stop!* I managed to prise his hand from the accelerator and thus kept the Luggie from damaging the vanity unit. I'd just added yet another bruise to my collection, that's all!

I should have cut my losses right there and headed back to the car, but no. We made our way back to the function. Out of the apartment, no problems. Over the road, still doing OK. Up the pathway and the ramp and just before the entry gate, Geoffrey went too far to the left instead of lining himself up with the middle of the gate, and he ended up with one back wheel in the garden. I managed to coax him to stand up, and I lifted the Luggie out of the garden. Geoffrey sat down, and I took command of the controls. I moved him backwards and then lined up the Luggie with the centre of the gateway.

Once we returned to the function, it was clear that I had, by then, missed my opportunity to view the new show apartment. *I'll just pop in one day through the week and visit it myself when I don't have Geoffrey with me*, I thought. As we munched on some yummy food, I noticed some people with whom I had chatted on another occasion. I made a move to go over and chat with them, but Geoffrey clearly did not want me to leave him. I gave up. *Let's just go now*, I decided, and I said that to Geoffrey. I helped him manoeuvre out of the space, and we headed towards the ramp in order to get back to the car.

Instead of turning towards the ramp, Geoffrey headed straight ahead at a good speed. I ran towards him shouting, "Geoffrey stop! Stop! You're going the wrong way. *Stop!* The steps are there, Geoffrey. *Stop!*" He was only about a metre short of the steps when the same lovely woman who'd helped me up from my fall earlier managed to indicate to Geoffrey to stop and he did.

Oh my God, what the hell am I doing? I can't manage this! I screamed internally.

Geoffrey turned the Luggie around, and we got to the car without any other incidents. But then he refused to park the Luggie away from the car and the kerb just a little in order to give himself room to get off of it. To get him up from the Luggie, I had to push myself into the garden and haul him up, then support him as he tried to move about where there was no space to do so. He almost tripped over the kerb as he then made his way to the passenger door.

Not only did he refuse to give himself or me any space to move in, he began to be abusive to me: It was all my fault. I was in his way. I should stop trying to control the Luggie. I should just let him do it, because he knew what he was doing. I was interfering. I was a nuisance. I should shut up and get out of the way (even though he could not get up without my help). He went on and on.

This abuse from Geoffrey was the last straw for me. I was furious, sad, frustrated, and overwhelmed all at once. On top of that, I was beginning to feel very sore from the fall. Emotionally, I fell headlong into a well of self-pity and sadness, and I found myself roaring a tirade of abuse right back at him. I was tired of being unappreciated. I'd had enough of having him fight me when all I wanted was to keep him safe. I had well and truly had enough, full stop.

I was cross with myself for not listening to my intuition and letting him come with me. I was cross with myself for buying the Luggie in the first place when it was clear that he no longer had the mental capacity to drive it or manoeuvre it safely—no reasoning ability, no planning ability, no spatial awareness, a disaster on wheels! There are no words to adequately explain my rage at him, at myself, and at the whole situation. I was trapped in a nightmare from which there was no escape, no salvation.

Suddenly, everything felt utterly hopeless and totally bleak. I once again had the screaming urge to plant my foot on the accelerator and slam us into a wall or a tree or anything I could find and kill us both right there and then. But I knew I could not do that to my family.

I very carefully drove us home, and then I hardly spoke to Geoffrey at all. I heated up some soup I'd cooked the day before, and when it was time for bed, I just went to bed. I did not ask him if he needed help. I did not help him off with his clothes or shoes. I heard him struggling, and I know it took him a long, long time to get undressed and into bed because I did not help him. He had said earlier that he didn't need me interfering, so I let him struggle. I was still so cross that I didn't care.

———————◆———————

The next morning, Geoffrey wouldn't wait for the carer to help him shower. He pulled himself into the shower by himself. His shower chair was around the wrong way, and his non-slip mat for the shower was upside down, rendering it useless. He grumped me away and wouldn't listen to me at all.

I burst into tears at the door when the care worker did arrive. I just felt lost, hopeless, totally overwhelmed, and miserable. She gave me a hug and took over Geoffrey with one fell swoop. He responded to her beautifully.

The care worker came back later, as scheduled, for two hours, and I headed off to a café. Just as I was leaving home, the lovely Bee sent me a text with hearts and emoji flowers. I phoned her as I was driving away from the house. My beautiful friend made time for me as I unloaded to her on the phone. By the time I arrived at the beach, I felt considerably better, but I was not out of the woods. I was very low and severely in need of time to myself and coffee in the sun. This was remedied by the beautiful cafe right on the beach.

I bought some cinnamon toast. I really needed a sugar hit, but I didn't want to send my blood sugar soaring either. I had taken my laptop with me, and as I unwound, I banged out some of my woes into this narrative.

Tamara phoned me, and once again, I had an opportunity to unload a bit. However, talking with Bee earlier had calmed me somewhat. Although I was still upset explaining to Tamara what had happened the night before and that morning, I was a bit more together. The sound of the waves and the beautiful sunshine also did a good job on me. I drove home with my inspirational songs belting out loudly on my car's speakers. I set my phone to select random songs, and some of them had a very strong *doof-doof* beat. I turned the volume up louder and sang along at the top of my lungs.

On the way home, I was waiting at some traffic lights with my music blaring when a young man pulled up beside me. Clearly, he could hear the extremely loud beat of my music. He looked over and was surprised when he saw that I was *not* a young chick, so he laughed and punched the air with a wink and a smile. It made me laugh—just what I needed.

It was time to reassess my normal way of being. Clearly, I had slipped back into feeling bad more often than I was feeling good.

Lyn phoned me that evening, and I was too upset to talk. She was wanting to include me in a Skype chat with our Melbourne family and friends, a group who were getting together the next day. I just said I'd talk to her tomorrow. When the next day came, we did do a Skype session, and it cheered me up a great deal.

———◆◆◆———

INSIGHT – THIRTEEN

How we are in our lives becomes normal to us. If we are used to reacting with anger to everything that happens around us, then that is normal for us. It's the usual. In our mind, we decide how we interpret the world or what we make things mean. Whether we believe that we are always overlooked or that we are always blamed for everything or that we never have enough money or any other regular thought or belief, we create our reality around that belief or thought. We find ways in our world to validate these thoughts or beliefs to make them true.

A simple example: If you think you are always in people's way, and you have experienced that in many situations in your life, then having someone mutter in annoyance when you've accidently bumped into each other will validate, yet again, that you are always in someone's way. This is how we create experiences to validate the belief.

Then what we tell ourselves becomes or remains a truth, the normal—when in fact, during that particular experience, the person who bumped into you could be feeling unwell, could have a headache, and may not have been looking where they were going. They might have been annoyed or just felt miserable. No matter the reason, you will see the situation through your normal responses or your normal expectations and validate your belief.

Another example is having a belief that you never have enough money. Then you might find yourself feeling bad every time a bill comes in or anytime you spend more from your wallet than you expected to spend. These are what's called our personal normal. What if this was not part of your normal? Like me, you might see that every time money is spent, it is simply making space in the wallet, purse, or bank account for more money to come in.

In our personal normal space, we will always interpret the world according to our past experiences and our reactions or responses to them. Our reactions to, responses to, and expectations of the world will usually look a particular way. Everyone's version of normal is a little different.

We are capable of creating a new kind of normal for ourselves. We don't have to be bound by our old realities, beliefs, or thoughts. Those are just habit, and often, they are not a true depiction of what is happening in your world. If your normal keeps you bound to the negative in any way, how about you consider changing your normal?

Ask yourself, "Am I happy in this situation? Are my thoughts making me happy? What am I focusing my energy and attention on? Is it good or not?" In any situation, especially when you are feeling hurt, upset, or annoyed with something or someone, ask yourself, "What am I making most important thing here?"

Imagine that someone has been rude and insulting to you. Most people will feel upset, slighted, or annoyed in some way. But how long do you hold on to those feelings? A few minutes? A day? A month? A year? Forever?

If you are making the need to feel slighted or hard done by the most important thing, you will hold on to those hurt feelings for a long time, because they will validate your beliefs about life. Sounds like a silly thing to do, but the payoffs can be varied. You might get to tell the story many times to different people, thus evoking self-righteous feelings within you. You might have people who want to take your side, and then the payoff might be that you get to feel important. You might also feel a sense of support from people, and this might validate your feeling of always being victimised, and that when you are a victim, you are looked after, supported, or cared for by others.

We are complex beings, and what goes on inside of each of us will be a little different. We will have many and varied reasons to hold on to negative feelings about ourselves or the situations which have occurred in our lives. Consider creating a new kind of normal for yourself. How would you prefer to feel most often in your life? What would life be like? How would you handle challenges?

Usually when I ask these types of questions, people answer that they would prefer to feel good and to handle life with ease, having only loving relationships and so forth. Then they add a *but* and go on to tell me all the reasons it can't be that way. All this says to me is that they are more committed to their bad feelings, thoughts, and beliefs—their normal—than they are to having an easy life. It's a simple equation: whatever you make most important will run your life.

In a new normal state, there are no excuses, no blame, no justifications, and no self-righteous reasons for holding on to any bad feelings. Creating a new normal for yourself means that the following are the most important things:

1. Trust that you are always looked after by God, spirit or the universe

2. Feel loved by yourself, by others, by God, spirit, or the universe

3. Allow support, assistance, and help: You do not need to do everything yourself or work everything out by yourself. It is OK and generous to ask for help.

4. Know that bad feelings held against others only hurts yourself, not them: Just allow the is-ness of things to be OK. Other people's opinions need not have any effect upon you.

5. Know that worrying is an exercise in uselessness: If you find yourself worrying, go back to the first point on this list.

When you are in your new normal state, you will be able to be happy, peaceful, and always in balance within yourself. There is no worry. There are no complaints or blaming anyone. There is no over-responsibility. You can make choices with ease and take action.

Living in this perspective, you will find that life flows. Almost like magic, God, spirit, and the universe will conspire to present amazing opportunities to you. Everything just gets better. It is a fantastic way to live your life, as you will be able to find joy in everything.

Allowing yourself to have a new normal isn't a single event. It is a process of reminding yourself and making new choices over and over. Trusting and knowing that you are valuable creates your new normal.

When things are not flowing well in your life and you are coming up against more and more difficulties, think about what you are making all of it mean about yourself and/or the world. Once you identify what you are making the most important thing, you can consciously choose to apply the five points listed above, and you can begin to turn things around in your favour. Sometimes it is emotionally quite difficult to give up feelings, beliefs, and habitual thoughts that have ruled your life. If this has not been working well for you, though, maybe it is well and truly time to think and believe differently and create new habitual thoughts which will improve your life.

When your body has had a jolt, an accident, or a fall, twenty-four hours later the soreness sets in, and I was sore—very, very sore. I climbed into bed, and the muscles around my diaphragm and ribs hurt a lot. As I first turned over, I groaned. Geoffrey asked me, what was wrong and, I replied that I was just sore, that's all.

"Sore from what?" he asked. He had totally forgotten that he had tripped me up and I'd crashed to the ground only a day ago. When I reminded him, all he said was, "Oh."

Bee phoned me to see how I was after my big download to her, and thankfully I was feeling a little better. I also really appreciated her checking in with me. I knew that I had been a support to her in the past, and it was really beautiful to know that the emotional support and caring went both ways.

The day after the Skype connection, both Carolyn and Jayma phoned me, again checking to see how I was. I felt loved and supported emotionally, even though there was nothing these beautiful beings could do physically for me. They were all in Melbourne. I nevertheless felt their love. It was good.

When Chris and Suzy phoned me, I was not able to chat for very long, as while we were talking, Geoffrey had an accident. The toilet floor was wet, his pants were wet, and even one shoe and sock were wet. I ended the call and helped him to undress and wash and re-dress. Then I cleaned up the mess on the floor. I thought that I felt OK about it, just tired. Actually, I felt a bit resigned, if I'm honest.

Thankfully, on the Monday, the Blue Care worker came, showered Geoffrey, and then stayed with him, which gave me time to get out. I went out and had a coffee and, once again, some healing sunshine and fresh air. I found that it took away some of the heaviness that I was feeling. I was still a long way away from my new normal feelings, however.

18

One night after I was in bed, Geoffrey was still wriggling around. Finally, he asked, "Can you pull me down?"

I asked him, "What do you want me to do?"

"Pull me down. I'm too high up the bed."

I told him to just wriggle himself down and that he was way too heavy for me to pull down the bed. In a confused voice, he said, "But I don't know how."

I literally had to tell him, slowly, step by step, what to do in order to move himself down the bed. It was funny as well as a bit sad.

———◆———

During a visit to our GP, she recommended that Geoffrey see a speech pathologist with regard to his continual choking problem. She sent a referral to the Robina Hospital outpatient department. Under normal circumstances, she would have sent him to have a gastroscope, but because of his heart problems, it was inadvisable for him to have a general anaesthetic.

The very next day, I received a call from the speech pathologist at the hospital. It was not to make an appointment; it was to inform me that Geoffrey was not eligible for an outpatient appointment because he had a home care package. Any speech pathology needed to be organised through his package manager and paid for from his package. First the oxygen and no electricity rebate, and now this. I was beginning to see some cracks in the home care package deal. It was frustrating.

I phoned the package manager at Blue Care and asked for a speech pathologist appointment. Then we just had to wait again.

At long last, the ramp for the back door arrived, along with a perfectly sized step for beside the bed. The step enabled Geoffrey to get into bed more easily, and the ramp made it far easier for him to access the back garden. Both of these relieved me considerably, because the way Geoffrey had been doing both these things certainly was dangerous. If he allowed assistance, it was not so bad. However, he would usually grump at me that he could do it by himself, even though he wobbled dangerously each time he tried to go outside.

Geoffrey could mostly still use the computer to listen to and watch YouTube videos. He loved to listen to relaxation music and various New Age artists. Sometimes, though, he would press the wrong key and become distressed. Then he would call out to me and tell me that the computer wasn't working properly.

I would have to jump up immediately and attend to this, no matter what else I might have been doing at the time, because he would, in his frustration, keep clicking things on the screen. This would overload the poor old computer, and it would lock up. I became very annoyed when this happened, because he would call me and then not wait until I came before he started bashing at the keyboard or clicking everything in sight. No amount of me explaining the uselessness of doing this would change his behaviour.

Geoffrey's computer died one day. No surprise, really. It didn't matter what we did—no visuals appeared on the screen. I attached another monitor, and it still didn't work. I removed the computer and replaced it with mine. We had purchased both computers at the same time quite a number of years earlier, but I found that as I used a laptop most of the time now, I was not fully utilising the main computer anymore. I removed all my important work from my desktop computer onto a new external hard drive before I gave it to Geoffrey to use.

I mistakenly thought that because the computers were exactly the same, he would cope with the changeover. What I had not thought about, though, was that my bookmarks bar was different than Geoffrey's, and because I hadn't had a chance to back up his settings before his computer died, I could not bring them over. He did not cope well with the fact that all of the bookmarks he had saved were not readily available on his new computer.

I had to take many deep breaths as I tried to show him that he would just have to do new searches to find his favourites again. I couldn't do it for him, as all he would tell me is what he didn't want, not what he did want. I tried, but it was another exercise in frustration and not worth the effort.

One day, when he was sitting in his comfortable chair, he called me to come to him. He vaguely said, "Slide. The sliding thing." He waved his hand vaguely in front of him. I had no idea what he was talking about or trying to say. He appeared to be looking straight ahead and out the window. I looked out the window and asked him if he was talking about something outside. "No!" was the sharp reply. He continued to wave vaguely in my direction.

"Do you want the TV on?" I asked.

"No!" he replied sharply.

"Do you want the computer on?" I tried.

"Yes, the slide thing," he said.

OK, I had a clue! I switched on the computer and waited until it booted up properly. Then I looked at him and asked, "What now?"

With a bit of back and forth between us, and with me having to interpret half words and nonspecific gestures, I discovered that he wanted YouTube up on the screen. I opened up one of his bookmarks and then looked at him and asked, "What do you want now? What slide thing?" By this time, I was having to control my annoyance and frustration.

Eventually, with a few more interactions, I discovered that he was referring to the volume slider on the screen below whichever video was playing. He swore that this slider control was not on his old computer. He strongly expressed that it was things like this which made this new computer all wrong. It was very different to *his* computer.

There was no use at all in explaining that it wasn't on the computer, it was part of YouTube on the internet, and that it was most definitely there when he used his old computer. In his reality, it wasn't there before, so I just agreed with him and commented that it was different, but it was just another volume control and nothing to worry about.

I returned to what I had been doing before he urgently called me to sort out the slide thing. I never worked out why it was so suddenly very urgent that I needed to attend to it immediately.

------◆------

Geoffrey began to complain of having an itchy back, and no amount of scratching would alleviate it. After a couple of days, despite applying soothing cream to it, I noticed that he had developed a rash which then began to spread to his stomach. I called the doctor's surgery but was unable to obtain an appointment for three days.

That night, he woke me and told me that he couldn't sleep because his rash was so itchy. Once I switched on the light and took a look, I saw that the rash had spread up his body and was now also on his chest and his forehead. Because I had no idea what could be causing this and thought it might be an allergic reaction to something, I was a bit worried that the next development might be a swollen tongue and throat. I took him to the hospital.

Of course, we waited for ages—two hours actually. That is the nature of going to an emergency department. It took another hour before Geoffrey was seen by a doctor. They had no idea what the rash was eventually decided that it was not dangerous. In checking all possibilities, they requested that Geoffrey produce a sample of urine. They gave me the specimen jar as well as a bottle to collect the rest of the urine.

Geoffrey could not manage to juggle this on his own. I put on some gloves, conveniently supplied on the wall of the hospital cubicle, and held the specimen jar in place. Then I waited. … and waited. I looked up at Geoffrey and saw that he was trying to let the flow happen, but nothing came out. I grinned as I asked if he had performance anxiety. He smiled and then, when I laughed out loud, giggled like a child and chuckled, "I think I do." Then he relaxed, and we were able to complete the task.

The doctor gave Geoffrey antihistamines and sent us home with a letter for the GP and instructions for us to continue with antihistamines at home. We got home at 5 a.m. I was shattered.

———◆———

Geoffrey's fingernails were becoming long, and he used to be able to cut and file them down himself. He could no longer do that. The podiatrist came to attend to his feet, and I asked her if she could also, on this occasion, trim his fingernails as well. I could do them for him, but I strongly dislike cutting nails, and I thought that as the podiatrist would have all the tools required, it'd be easy. No! Of course not. It was another process for which we would have to make a request through our home care package manager.

Oh my God! Why wasn't anything simple? Why couldn't I just get help with something without having to go through all these damn processes? I decided that I would cut his nails myself and just deal with my discomfort. However, the following Monday, Geoffrey had a new carer who would be coming every two weeks. The first time he came, after he helped Geoffrey shower, the carer also cut Geoffrey's nails. Oh, how wonderful!

———◆◆◆———

I was keeping up with the washing fairly well. With the laundry off the kitchen, I found it easy to wash and hang out the clothes. Because the laundry was close to where I usually was in the house, I could hear the beep of the machine when it finished, and then I'd hang things out to dry. It sounds silly, but I found that if I didn't hear that sound, I totally forgot that I'd put washing on. Maybe dementia is catching?

And plenty of washing, there most certainly was! Some days, Geoffrey would wet his pants at the toilet because he hadn't arrived there in time, and he would wet everything as he pulled his pants down. Sometimes I found that I was taking his shoes off, changing his pull-ups and his trackpants, and putting his shoes back on several times a day. Then the floor needed to be mopped each time. I think that on the days that his brain was more out of gear, he didn't realise that he needed to go to the toilet until it was too late.

We had more computer problems and communication problems. Often Geoffrey wouldn't or couldn't tell me what he wanted or what it was that he couldn't find, but he just kept telling me what he *didn't* want. This made it difficult to understand him. It was hard to meet his needs when he became frustrated and I didn't understand him. At this time, he was communicating in very short sentences or single words, often accompanied by non-direct waving gestures. It was like playing charades, only a lot less fun.

Was it because he had no breath? Was it just his brain deterioration? Or was it both? I didn't know. When I was tired, I yelled at him and gave up. I decide that I needed to work out how to download some of what he liked, and then he could just listen to it. I think the computer was beyond him now, but *he* thought that he was fine, it was just the stupid computer!

The oxygen got used a fair bit through the day; he didn't seem to need it so much at night if he had used it through the day. The oxygen converter sat in the lounge, which was in the middle of the house. The hose, although quite long, did not reach everywhere, as the house was large. It reached to the bed for night-time use and to Geoffrey's comfortable chair in the family room. It did not reach to the table in the casual meals area, though. If Geoffrey was using the oxygen and wished to sit at the table, I either left the converter in the lounge and pulled it a bit closer towards the kitchen and then pulled the meals table a little towards the lounge, or I unplugged the converter and moved the whole thing into the family-room/kitchen area. Either way, Geoffrey could use the oxygen at the table.

Geoffrey would sometimes become cross if I didn't give him choices, so I did make an effort to check in with him whenever practical. One day I asked him, "Where do you want to sit to have lunch? In your chair or at the table?" As I asked him this, I also used gestures to indicate the choices, and I spoke slowly in order to give him time to process the choices. I watched him and asked again, "At your chair or at the table?"

The response I got was a vague waving of the hand, and I heard him say, "It doesn't."

I looked around and tried to work out what he meant. I repeated the question.

He made a herrumph noise, waved his hand again, and said, "Umm, it ... umm, won't! ... air."

From that, I deduced that he had worked out that the air hose from the oxygen converter wouldn't reach to the table.

"That's OK," I said. "I'll sort that out if you want to sit at the table. You just have to answer the question of where you want to sit. I will sort the rest out. You don't need to solve the problem. That's my job!"

He just looked blankly at me.

"So, do you want to sit at the table?" I asked.

He nodded. I helped him up from the chair and moved the machine into the family room. He finally sat at the table. He had his oxygen. He had his lunch. Such a simple thing was no longer simple.

Geoffrey was forgetting to flush the toilet. Doesn't sound like much of a problem, but it was annoying and unhygienic. There was nothing I could do about it, and I had to learn to just check the toilets regularly and flush them myself if and when they needed it.

19

It was several weeks after getting and accepting the quote for the ramp at the back door and the step for next to the bed before they arrived. I welcomed them, as Geoffrey was having trouble getting into bed and was seriously dangerous when he went out the back door, down the step.

Although I was feeling a bit happier within myself, I was still weary. The care of someone with dementia plus a heart condition was constant and relentless. I had done some research into the cost of permanent residential care. It appeared to be a complicated process: researching, finding a place suitable to care for him and his needs, inspecting different care homes, applying, and being put on a waiting list.

And then there was the financial side of things. Centrelink would need to do a new asset test on us and work out what Geoffrey's share of everything would be. If his share was more than $48,500, we would be asked to pay a weekly fee as well as a percentage of Geoffrey's pension (which would be a single person's pension). Given that I would no longer be eligible for the carers pension and would essentially have little or no income, I'd be eating into our meagre savings. Oh great! I didn't think I could afford to have Geoffrey in permanent residential care.

Physically, Geoffrey was becoming weaker. He could do with a wheelchair for when we were out of the house. I'd been seating him on his wheelie-walker and pushing him around when we went out. This was not ideal, but the Luggie was a dangerous weapon as driven by him. We didn't go to the market that week because he wasn't with it enough to be safe on the Luggie. I wasn't sure where we went from there. Because Geoffrey needed help with showering and the higher funded package had not come through yet, there was not enough money left in his package for a wheelchair at that time.

Dear Darryl suggested a GoFundMe page to pay for some of those extras for Geoffrey, like a wheelchair, and/or to support me. I had a hissy fit when he suggested it. A bunch of thoughts went through my head: *Why would anyone want to contribute to us? Don't waste your energy, because no one would contribute. There are many more worthy causes out there.* Darryl suggested that we could get in touch with people who had done our courses and classes in the past who would have benefitted from our input and assistance. I said that the answer was probably no, but I'd think about it.

A couple of weeks later, Darryl was in Brisbane for work purposes, and he travelled down to the Gold Coast to spend an afternoon and have dinner with us. The topic came up, of course. He reminded me that Geoffrey and I had helped many, many people over the years, and maybe it was time to let people give back to us. My tears flowed, and I tried very hard to take this mad idea off the table. Eventually, though, I agreed. I thought that it wouldn't matter if no one contributed. We'd be no worse off than we were now, and who knows? It might work and help us out.

It was good to have a flow of visitors from Melbourne, as all of them contributed to me in their own unique way. Catherine had a conference to attend in Lennox Head (Northern New South Wales), and she stayed with us for two days before the conference and two days afterwards. It was not only good to have people to chat to, it was extremely validating for me to have other people see how Geoffrey was. It was not my imagination. He was deteriorating.

I was juggling the finances, and Geoffrey never enquired about anything financial at all. When our water filter broke—it was very old—I purchased a new under-sink system which, although expensive, could be moved to the new apartment when it was ready. I felt as though as soon as I managed to tuck away a little money, something occurred which required a lump of it. Usually whatever the cost, it was fairly well what I had saved. I had to look at this as being looked after, as I always had the money needed at the time. Occasionally, I went down the rabbit hole of *Oh dear, I've just emptied the bank account*, but usually I could be sensible and see that there was always money available for whatever came up.

I was feeling weary. Looking after Geoffrey and the household and the shopping and the bills and the appointments felt very constant and a big commitment. Some days, when Geoffrey was very vague, it was most definitely more difficult. He still would continually accuse me of not telling him things. I was almost at the stage of not bothering to tell him anything, because he very rarely remembered anyway. But sometimes he did remember, so I kept telling him stuff.

I always wrote the week's activities on the whiteboard, and sometimes he read it and sometimes he didn't. He would accuse me of not telling him what was going to happen or who was coming or where we had to go, even though it was written on the board right there for him to see. There was no logic.

He questioned me when I went out for a couple of hours on a Monday or whenever I had a Blue Care carer looking after him. He didn't understand that I needed to get out and away from him sometimes; otherwise, I felt suffocated. I did really enjoy my two hours off, even if all I did was sit with a coffee in a cafe and write. Usually I was as vague as I could be when Geoffrey asked where I was going, but I did feel a bit guilty about my need to get away when all he wanted to do was spend time with me.

Over the next few weeks, he improved somewhat, but it was only obvious on some days. Mostly, he was struggling to string more than two words together at a time, and sometimes it was only half a word with vague hand-waving gestures. When his girls phoned him to wish him happy Father's Day, he could barely speak. He strained to find words and then just mumbled out what he could. It was sad to watch.

———◆———

There's no doubt that looking after someone in Geoffrey's condition was challenging. It was a full-time job, and because there were many things that Geoffrey used to help with or do which he now could not, there was a lot on my plate. The everyday things were a given:

- making the meals and snacks
- shopping, doing the dishes
- making the appointments
- driving to wherever was needed
- getting Geoffrey's wheelie-walker in and out of the car
- changing the sheets
- doing the washing/laundry
- hanging out and bringing in the washing
- managing the money
- paying the bills.

Then there were all the extras:

- turning the oxygen converter on or off several times a day as required
- getting Geoffrey's medications and supplements and ensuring he took them, often picking up the ones he dropped on the floor

- helping to clean his face up after eating or drinking
- helping him to dress and undress on the days that he didn't have help from a Care Worker to shower, including on and off with the pull-ups and disposing of them
- extra cleaning of the toilets and toilet floors (sometimes a few times a day)
- helping him to sit at the table properly
- helping him when he became confused at the computer
- helping with the iPad when he forgot how to use it or how to turn it off
- helping with the TV remote control when he forgot how to use it
- answering all the questions, often the same questions again and again
- ensuring everything that was in the diary was written on the whiteboard
- ensuring Geoffrey was ready to leave in time when we had to go out
- keeping him safe whenever possible

There was more, of course. It was just life. That's how it was for me at that time.

On the days when Geoffrey was not so well, I was up and down all day to attend to his needs. I was still struggling with depression on and off. It depended upon the day. Some days I had plenty of energy, and I was able to care for him with genuine love and compassion. Other days, it felt demanding and grim, and I was continually anxious that he was going to have a heart attack every other moment. Sometimes I could swing either way within a day. It was a battle to shift the low feelings, as it felt as though this was going to go on forever, and I felt very tied down. I tried my best not to sit in that low state and to lift myself back to my new normal state of trusting and loving and feeling happy.

———————✦•✦•✦———————

On 1 September 2018, Geoffrey had a fall as he was getting back into bed in the early hours of the morning. I just heard the crash and bang as he hit the window and the blinds. Thank goodness, the glass was safety glass and didn't break.

I jumped out of bed and discovered Geoffrey on the floor between the bed and the window. Although I was going to put a chair there for Geoffrey to help himself up with, he was lying very awkwardly, and it took me a while to help him to physically move his body into a position whereby he could get onto his knees and then, with my help, use the chair to lever himself up. Fortunately, he only bruised his bottom, as he had scraped it on the edge of the new step as he went down. He had no idea how it happened, and I guessed that he must have just lost his balance.

The speech pathologist visited Geoffrey and came up with some good ideas on how to limit the number of coughing fits he was having. Some things I was doing already, such as getting him to use a straw for regular drinks. Other ideas were new. Whether I could get Geoffrey to do all these things or not was another matter.

She explained about the mechanics of swallowing and encouraged Geoffrey to do some swallowing with no food or drink. He found it impossible to do in the way that she explained. She wanted him to do a hard swallow and to really work those muscles in order to make them stronger. Geoffrey looked at her blankly, and although she demonstrated with very clear instructions and extremely well-defined facial and body cues, Geoffrey was still unable to do it. Oh well, we'd just have to do the best we could with what we had.

We still had some amusing things from time to time: One day, as I gave Geoffrey a hug, he let out a big burp in my ear. I looked at him with mock shock on my face. He said, "Well, you squeezed it out of me." Then he giggled like a kid.

20

Tamara came up from Melbourne to stay for nine days, which helped a lot. It was not only delightful to have her company; it was great that it wasn't only me who was jumping up to attend to Geoffrey all the time. In general, I'd been feeling very trapped. For example, I'd had a number of people telling me that I would enjoy seeing a particular film which was showing at the cinema. It was truly a good idea, but one which I felt was impossible. I felt very confined, as I thought I had no chance of doing that. Geoffrey wouldn't have managed it, and there was not enough time for me to do that in the hours I had respite on Mondays or Fridays.

I loved my Thursday mornings at art, but in order to do anything, something had to go. On the Thursday, Tamara and I went to the cinema. Oh, how I enjoyed it! The film was superb, and I had a few good belly laughs and continued to giggle about it for days afterwards. What a treat!

The following weekend, Fiona and the children came down from the Sunshine Coast. It always lifted my heart to see them. There was nothing like grandchildren to lift my spirits.

Although Tamara had to be at the airport by midday on the Sunday, we still managed to have a lovely time together. The weather was warm, and the pool was a lovely 31 degrees, so we had a great time in the water. The children, now 5 and 7 years old, were like little fish in the water. I did have to manage Geoffrey as well as I could, but we had lunch out at a cafe on the beach on the Saturday, then the girls and the children walked and rode along the foreshore together. It was terrific that they had a little time together, and Geoffrey and I went home for a nap/rest.

On the Sunday, we all went to the farmers market and had breakfast by the lake. Just beautiful! Geoffrey was pushed in a wheelchair, as it was too much effort for him to walk around the market with his wheelie-walker.

One thing which was a little difficult was trying to keep Geoffrey doing the right thing in front of the children, especially at mealtime. Geoffrey's table manners had gone out the window, so to speak. He waved his fork in the air, he picked up things with his fingers, he dribbled, and he often took his dentures out during the meal. The kids also had a bit of a giggle when Pa was wearing a big bib at mealtimes, but we managed to avert any real disasters.

My granddaughter, did come into our bedroom on one of the mornings and Geoffrey was only half dressed. When she saw Geoffrey wearing pull-ups, which look just like a toddlers' nappy only much bigger, she giggled and giggled and thought it was the most hilarious thing she'd ever seen. Geoffrey had his attention on something else and didn't notice. Oh, well, that's life!

———◆———

I felt very lonely on the Monday. It was just Geoffrey and me. I had no one to chat to, and I felt isolated. I suppose I half expected that. I thought I'd be prepared, but it snuck in like a bad smell, and I felt myself sinking somewhat rather than being peaceful and happy. I had to work very hard internally to pull myself up to feeling OK again, but I did eventually manage it.

Geoffrey was picking up a little physically, and he was talking a little better too. That didn't mean that he always made sense. It was *so* frustrating trying to have a conversation with him. Between him forgetting words, being unable to make decisions, and forgetting stuff, it was always a battle, and I had to have a thick layer of patience on.

We had various days where Geoffrey would ask me, "What day is it today?" Then, later, "Is it Tuesday today?" Then, "It's Tuesday today, isn't it?" Then, "What day is it today?" Each time, I just answered the question.

Tamara had downloaded some apps for me to be able to access all the TV programs on the iPad. I'd told her that I was thoroughly sick of having the same programs on TV over and over. Geoffrey would want to watch the same things again and again. It did not matter that they were all repeated and repeated.

So while he watched TV, I could now sit next to him with headphones on, watching programs that I liked on the iPad. The trouble with this was that it brought his attention to the iPad, and he started to want to use it through the day. Try as he might, he always needed help with it. He had never learned how to use it when his mental capacity was good, so now it was a total disaster.

He didn't know how to open YouTube, so I'd point out the app and show him. After a while, he would accidentally initiate Siri, and then he would get confused when Siri's suggestions would appear on the screen when he failed to ask her anything.

"How do I get rid of this stupid thing?" he'd call out to me. I'd have to attend to it and get him back to wherever he was, usually listening to YouTube music.

"How do I turn this up/down?" he'd yell. I had to jump quickly to him, or else he'd yell it out again. I pointed out the sound level switch at the side of the device over and over, but he never remembered this.

"How do I turn this thing off?" was the next request called out. It didn't matter how many times he used the iPad, he was never able to remember how to use it, but he still wanted to use it and continued to yell out his needs with it.

One time, I was outside gathering in the washing off the line. When I went back inside, he had worked himself up into a lather because there was something he wanted to do on the iPad, but it "wasn't working" again, and I hadn't come when he called. *Oh dear,* I thought. *How dare I try to do anything else except attend to him?*

———◆—◆———

Now that it was mid-September and the weather was warmer in the mornings, I resumed taking Lyn to hydrotherapy on Tuesdays. Paul would bring Lyn over in her car, and I'd drive that to the pool and back. Paul would stay with Geoffrey; they'd go down the road for coffee, and he'd take my car. It worked well, as Lyn didn't need to change cars, and Geoffrey didn't need to try to get in and out of a car that was lower than he was used to.

What I forgot the first day that we resumed this routine was that it had been some months since Paul had looked after Geoffrey, and Geoffrey had deteriorated. Geoffrey told Paul that he only needed his stick to walk, and Paul believed him, because in the past, it would have been OK. Paul did find that he had to hold on to Geoffrey's other arm, as Geoffrey was quite unstable.

The next week, I made sure to explain to Paul that Geoffrey *must* use his wheelie-walker everywhere he went and that Paul was the boss, not Geoffrey. I said to him that he couldn't believe everything that Geoffrey said. I reminded him that Geoffrey had dementia.

I could understand Paul's predicament completely, as he was used to taking care of Lyn, who had rheumatoid arthritis; she needed help with all the physical things, but her mind was on the ball. Geoffrey was very different. I just forgot sometimes that I had to keep others up to date with how Geoffrey was because I'd become used to the changes. Others didn't always notice them immediately.

INSIGHT - FOURTEEN

We see the world as we expect to see it. More often than not, we see things and people as we have always seen them. This is why people will miss changes, which may be subtle, until they are blindingly obvious.

Every day, we are bombarded with an enormous amount of sensory information. In order to function in the world, our brains learn to ignore thousands of these sensory messages, only focusing on the things which seem to be most important. We can notice this when we go somewhere new and there are so many things to see and hear that it fills us with wonder and amazement. After we have been back to that same place many times, we don't really see or notice everything; it has become known to our senses, so our brain largely ignores it. Then we have plenty of brainpower to focus on tasks or conversations and so on.

So when something happens or something changes, you might not be aware of it immediately. You have probably had the experience of knowing that something has changed, but you are not quite sure what it was. If your friend has a haircut, for example, it may or may not be immediately obvious to you because you're just used to your friend however she might be. Partly this is because you've stopped looking and noticing.

Perhaps it is you who has changed. Maybe you have lost weight, for example, and you've been surprised at how many people haven't noticed. It's not that they don't care; it's often because they are your friends, and they accept you for you, and they are used to you as you have been. Their brain doesn't take in the changes or make the small changes matter enough to notice. Sometimes the difference has to be dramatic before their brain allows them to notice.

The same can be said of looking after someone with dementia. You can become so used to dealing with them as they have been that, if the changes are slow and subtle, it's not always immediately obvious that you need to respond to them a little differently.

In general, we see the world as we are used to seeing it and how we believe it to be, whether this is physically with our eyes or with our emotions. For example, if you have been told that dogs are dangerous—or you have, in the past, had a scary experience with a dog—then you could believe and see all dogs as dangerous. With this fear in place within you, dogs evoke that fear every time you see one. This can bring about exactly what you fear, as dogs will sense your fear and will sometimes react to it, and you could create exactly what you fear.

Living with a greater awareness allows you to see the is-ness of every situation. You can respond accordingly, appropriately, and with a greater sense of generosity to yourself and others.

21

The garage door was still not done. Every time I saw it, it annoyed me. It had been hard to get people to come and quote for it. They either didn't return my enquiry call or didn't turn up to quote, or did come over and then didn't ever send a quote.

I phoned one more place, and it looked promising. I crossed my fingers. It was stupid things like this which contributed to my stress level. It just seemed like there were always so many little things to be done. I could allow these things to pull me down into apathy; then I got the "can't be bothered", and nothing proceeded.

⎯⎯⎯◆⎯⎯⎯

Two of Geoffrey's lower front teeth broke off. He had full dentures on the top and partial lower dentures with seven of his own teeth left at the lower front. I wasn't sure whether it was going to be worth it to take him to the dentist. He wanted to go, as it was bothering him, and he seemed to be most incapable of leaving it alone. His tongue became irritated as he continually rubbed his tongue over the broken teeth.

We weren't sure whether the dentist would rebuild the teeth or pull the remains of the teeth out. Either way, I knew it would be an expensive exercise.

Another tooth broke before we went to the dentist, and then we discovered that yet another tooth was about to break also. The dentist suggested that all four teeth be removed a few days later. Geoffrey was to have a large dose of antibiotics an hour prior to the teeth coming out. Geoffrey appeared to understand what needed to happen.

It was also suggested that we get Geoffrey's lower dentures altered before the teeth come out, so that there were some teeth over the top of the removed ones. We went to the dental technician, and he assured me I could pick up the altered dentures before Geoffrey had the teeth removed.

It was a busy week as I took Geoffrey to the different appointments. The dentist had to work quite hard to get the rest of Geoffrey's rotten teeth out, and the next day Geoffrey had a huge bruise on his chin. It was very purple, and it looked as though he'd been in a big punch-up! Thank goodness we had the adjusted lower dentures for him to put in. He'd had to have three stitches, and he was not able to stop himself from having his tongue worrying the area constantly. With the lower dentures in, the area was covered, and his tongue was unable to reach those injured gums.

I had to prepare all meals mashed up, as he was unable to bite food at all. This I found difficult after a while, as I was running out of ideas. Fortunately, Geoffrey was happy with soup or smoothies a lot of the time.

We would have to get new lower dentures in a number of weeks when the gums had healed and shrunk down. The whole teeth thing cost a lot of money, and I was glad that I'd saved up some in reserve so that it didn't cause any stress for me.

I noticed at this time that Geoffrey's fine-motor skills had deteriorated. He struggled to find the right button on the TV remote, not just because he'd forgotten how to use it but because he was unable to get the correct finger to do what he needed it to do. He was unable to mash his own banana. He just didn't have the strength in his hands anymore.

Each time carers came, they clearly said hello to Geoffrey and introduced themselves or reintroduced themselves. He often didn't know their names even if they had been many times before, and it wasn't until someone had been regularly for a long time that he would remember the name.

When it was time for Geoffrey's review with the cardiologist, we were told that he needed a new current referral from the GP. Personally, I didn't understand why on earth he needed a new referral every year, but that was the system. Our GP was away for a couple of weeks, so the cardiologist appointment had to be put back until I could get a GP appointment.

Then I realised that we'd need a double appointment because there was all the paperwork to be filled out for Geoffrey's respite stay as well. The respite stay was fast approaching, as I was headed to Melbourne at the end of October. Nothing seemed simple. Everything seemed to have extra conditions attached to it or needed some extra action. It added somewhat to my overwhelmed feeling.

During one of the Sundays we went to the market, Geoffrey charged off in front of me on his Luggie as we headed back to the car. He was going at some speed, and I could not catch up to him. I saw him head off in the wrong direction but could do nothing about it. Not once did he look around to see if I was behind him, with him, or anywhere near him. Nor did he realise that he was travelling much faster than I could walk (or run for that matter).

There it was again: lack of awareness. I had no way of knowing if he would realise his error or if he'd get to the end of the path and have no idea at all of where he needed to go to get back to the car. In my annoyance, I followed him all the way up the wrong way, all the way to the end of the path. I caught up to him, and by then I was furious. I knew that there was no point in being cross, but I was tired and very pissed off. I roared like a fishwife and berated him for charging off without me. I knew it was a useless thing to do, but I just had to let off some steam.

Again, I was miserable. I felt as though our lovely morning had been spoilt. I knew that he had just done what he'd done with no thought. That's what happens with dementia. I guess that at some level, though, I kept hoping that he'd be normal, react normally, have some normal awareness, or be considerate of me like normal.

Because Geoffrey was somewhat stronger physically again, he thought, with his dementia brain, that he could walk about without his walker. To say that it was dangerous for him to be doing this was an understatement. He was still very wobbly, and I often found him lurching from his walker to somewhere else. He'd get grumpy with me if I stopped him, grabbed the walker, and put it back in front of him.

"I'm OK," he'd grump. "I don't need you interfering!"

The truth was that he was not OK doing this, and many times he barely escaped falling. In his mind, he was better and could walk by himself. In working with someone with dementia, I'd been told to work with *their* reality, but when he was doing something dangerous, it was a bit more difficult.

I tried explaining to him that if he fell and broke his leg, he'd end up in hospital and might not be able to come home. I wouldn't be able to look after him, and he'd have to go into care. In that moment, he got it. Five minutes later, though, he had forgotten it and was lurching around again. It was hard not to be frustrated.

One day, I discovered Geoffrey's gold ring on the floor of the family room. Three days later, he asked me if I knew where his ring was. I supposed that at least he did eventually remember or realise that it was not on his finger. I didn't give it back to him, because he had lost weight, and in order for it to be safe on his finger again, I'd need to get it resized. That was another job which I wasn't sure if I'd get around to or not.

Geoffrey's birthday was coming up. I knew he'd prefer to go out for lunch rather than dinner, so I asked him if there was anywhere special he wanted to go. We were planning for Lyn and Paul to come with us, and Chris and Terry were up from Melbourne at the time. We both thought it'd be lovely for them to be able to join us.

"It's that place in Burleigh," he said. He couldn't tell me what it was called or exactly where it was. I enquired as to whether it was a club or a pub. No amount of prompting helped, except he did insist that it was a club. He clearly had a place in mind, but he was totally unable to describe it or to tell me the name of it or where it was or what it was near. All he said was that it was just off the highway.

I thought hard, and other than two surf clubs and a bowls club, I couldn't think of another club in Burleigh that it might be. He was emphatic that it wasn't those but that it was definitely a club. We had never been there together, but he had been there on one of his weekly bus trips.

The next day we had to go down to Tweed to get his hearing aid settings reviewed. I suggested that we might return via the highway. I could drive up past Burleigh, and he might be able to show me where he thought this club was off the highway. Once I knew what it was called, I could book us seats for Friday for the six of us.

"No, just phone and make the booking," he barked at me.

"How can I phone when I don't know what the place is?" I said.

"Anyone can just phone. Anyone would know," he growled.

"How, if I don't know the name of the place?"

"Just use the phone and call them!" he insisted.

"But who do I call?"

"Anyone will know. You could ask anyone. Anyone would know," he repeated.

I was becoming frustrated. "Well, *I* don't know who to phone, cos you can't tell me exactly what it is. Now you say it is not a surf club but it *is* a club, and that it is somewhere north of Burleigh. Well, unless you know what it is and not just what it isn't, I have no idea who to phone," I grumped back at him. I threw the phone at him and said sharply, "*You* phone the place, since you think it's that easy."

"I can't use this thing," he said airily as he tossed the phone back at me.

I had some very uncharitable thoughts and no idea where to go from there.

In a little-boy voice, he said, "OK, just forget it. Don't bother."

"What do you mean, *don't bother*? You said you want to go somewhere specific for lunch. Oh God, you are a shit. You are driving me totally nuts."

I hate this nonsense, I thought. *I just can't deal with this. I'm trying to help you.*

"*You* were the one who came up with a suggestion of where you wanted to go," I pointed out. "Now I'm making another suggestion so that you might be able to work out what the bloody place is! It's for *you*, you bloody shit. All I'm offering is a possible solution. Don't tell me to forget it in that tone of voice, or I'll be shoving your birthday lunch up your arse!"

Not nice of me, for sure, but I truly was frustrated. He said nothing.

I took a deep breath and started again. "What's wrong with just driving to the area, and you can see if you recognise something? If we can't find it, we'll just book a table at either Burleigh Surf Club or North Burleigh Surf Club, OK?"

By then, I was dreading not only driving around the next day but the damn birthday lunch. I didn't know why I bothered. Why did I even try to do something nice for the big ratbag?

On the way to Tweed, we travelled along the motorway, and despite the fact that Geoffrey had insisted that the place he wanted to go to was off the highway and it was a club, he indicated a turn-off from the motorway. It turned out that where he wanted to go was the West Burleigh *Pub*, not a club, not off the highway, not somewhere I'd never been, because Geoffrey and I had most definitely been there before. I just sighed.

Thank God the birthday lunch went well. The fact that I actually had a glass of wine probably helped.

22

Our friends Julie and John were up from Melbourne visiting relatives, and they came to stay for two nights. Those couple of days lifted my spirits enormously. I always had a good laugh with Julie; we have the same mad sense of humour. I knew I was very fortunate to have such beautiful friends.

Geoffrey was just the same with the TV remote control. Usually he didn't consider me; he would just change the channel whenever it suited him. But he did it to John also! Dear sweet John didn't say a thing. He just watched TV with Geoffrey no matter what Geoffrey did with the controls.

Julie and I were doing 5D diamond paintings in the dining room on the table. I dropped almost a whole pack of about 1,500 tiny tiles, 2.8 mm to be precise, onto the shag pile carpet. Julie and I dived under the table and tried to pick them all up. We ended up laughing our heads off. It was hilarious fun. We were hot and sweaty and giggling like schoolgirls. It made my week! Thank you, Julie. I love you, my beautiful friend.

It was impossible sometimes trying to communicate with Geoffrey. He would say something, and when I responded, he would be confused. When I would explain to him and reiterate what he had said in the first instance, he would reply that no, he hadn't said that. Then I would realise that I was attempting to be logical. I just had to let it go each time because there was no logic.

The week after Julie and John went home, I had a sore throat, then a cough, then *OMG, I'm sick!* Geoffrey couldn't do anything to help me. My head was pounding, and my body was sore. My diaphragm hurt when I coughed.

On the Friday, Geoffrey had a doctor's appointment in order to get a new referral for the cardiologist, get some scripts, and fill in paperwork for respite. The receptionist had only put in a single appointment, even though when I booked it, I had asked for a double appointment. There was no way our lovely GP doctor could do all this in fifteen minutes! While we were there, she gave me a script for antibiotics. By Monday, I'd given in and got the script filled.

That evening, Geoffrey did try to help by emptying the dishwasher, but he just put dishes and cups on the benchtops. He didn't remember where everything went, so I still had to put everything away. All weekend, I dragged myself around, and Geoffrey was totally unaware of my pain and discomfort, even though I was coughing up mucous with a hacking sound. I felt like a wreck.

As the weekend dragged on, I was just so sore. My sinuses hurt, and my head was pounding. I took two paracetamol and some ibuprofen, something I'd hardly ever resorted to, but it was the only way I could be upright for any length of time. I also made sure to have lots of Vitamin C, my herbal cold and flu tabs, and my Chinese herbal sinus pills. Nevertheless, I felt awful. Geoffrey failed to notice.

On the Sunday morning, Geoffrey grumbled to me, "Come on, get up, you're not *that* sick."

Oh my God, I felt ghastly, and he was very lucky I was too sick to take his head off!

I struggled to shake off the hopeless feeling while I was sick. No matter how many times I reminded Geoffrey to use the brakes on his walker before he sat down on it, he would still sit on it, and it would move away from him as he sat down. He would still wobble across the room without holding on to anything. It was so dangerous, but he would get cross if I said anything, so I decided to give up. There was just no point in telling him over and over. I decided that if he fell, it was not my fault.

I was feeling a bit resigned. It was like continually pushing back the tide. There was just no point in trying. I knew that I was never going to make a difference. He was *so* stubborn and *so* unaware and *so* illogical that there was just no point anymore. I felt that I just had to give up. I just could *not* keep telling him; he was never going to remember. I had to stop taking an excess amount of responsibility for him. If he hurt himself, then so be it. I had to allow the risk.

It was impossible to keep him totally safe from himself. I did my best to ignore when he wobbled around without holding on to anything, ignore his messy eating habits, and ignore the unsafe way he did things. I had to make it not matter or else I'd go nuts. I was worn out. No matter what I said or did, he was still going to do these things.

I was really looking forward to having time in Melbourne with my friends, my family, and my beautiful soul family, and not having to give any thoughts to Geoffrey's needs because he would be in respite care. A soul family is a small community of like-minded people, but more than that, they kept me sane. They sent messages of love and support; sent me hugs and gave real hugs when I saw them; seriously cared about each other; were connected at a deep soul level; had similar goals and supported and assisted each other in achieving them; and stayed in communication with each other.

One morning, as I sat on the toilet, Geoffrey needed me to put his hearing aids in, so he came into the bathroom, sat less than a metre away from me, and waited. He had no thought of that being inappropriate or that I might like some privacy for a few minutes. Yes, everything needed to be explained to him. It was very childlike of him, and I found that there were many things which needed to be explained, or he had to be guided in some way with a number of situations because he had lost the ability to respond in socially appropriate ways.

The package manager advised me that because Geoffrey was needing more care, he was close to running out of funds each month. He suggested that until his level four package came through, we call My Aged Care and get approval for top-up funding through Commonwealth Home Support. I then told Liberty that from November, Geoffrey would be funded from the Community Home Support Program, and next year he would probably have one day outing on the bus and another day in the centre. I knew Geoffrey didn't understand, but I needed it. It just meant that we would have to contribute a small amount each week towards the cost. I could cope with that.

The package manager also suggested that we apply for the Continence Aids Payment Scheme. This was a government-funded scheme whereby we were given a grant twice a year in order to pay for continence products. For this, we needed Geoffrey to be assessed by a continence nurse and forms needed to be completed—of course! We went to our GP, who then sent a referral to Oz Care to arrange for the continence nurse to come. Unfortunately, when the appointment time finally arrived, Geoffrey was in hospital, and I needed to call Oz Care again to rebook. I didn't actually get around to this until the New Year.

During that visit to the doctor, she explained to Geoffrey what the "end of life choices" forms that I had filled out meant. She had to sign the paperwork off, and she wanted to give Geoffrey an understanding of what it was all about. She explained it very eloquently and in language which would be clear to Geoffrey. Then she asked him if he could explain it back to her to see if he understood. I'm sure he understood, but he was unable to repeat it or explain any of it back to her. There was nothing in there which Geoffrey and I had not discussed years ago when his cognitive function was more normal, so I was not worried.

———— ◆•◆•◆ ————

The weekend before I was off to Melbourne and Geoffrey was to go into respite, I packed. It doesn't sound like a big deal, but I was still coughing badly, which exhausted me. I had to make sure that everything of Geoffrey's was named. Some things were named already from the last stay, but there were different clothes that he wanted to take this time, so they had to be named.

I managed to name everything without a single name label to spare. I made a mental note to order some more name tags for future use. He had to take his own pull-ups, his own over-toilet chair, and the oxygen converter—named, of course. I had already had his medications packed by the pharmacy which usually look after the medications for that aged care home so that we didn't get the problems with the medications we'd had in March.

Then I had to pack for my Melbourne trip, which I found difficult because the weather was so different to what I had become used to. For example, at that time of year, late October, our overnight temperature usually didn't drop below 18 degrees centigrade, and in Melbourne, if you were lucky, it would get *up* to 18 with some intermittent days of up to 25, but the overnight temperature was more like 6 to 8. Brrrr!

The week before I went to Melbourne, Geoffrey seemed to have a cognitive decline. He didn't know what day it was; he'd look at the whiteboard to see what was going on and then ask me five minutes later about something that he expected was happening that day but was in fact a couple of days ahead. He would make a statement about something, and when I replied or asked him what he meant because I didn't understand the question, he'd get confused. If I reminded him of what I thought he'd said, he'd growl, "No I didn't." I'd have to just let it go because he'd forgotten already what he'd said that started the conversation.

One morning, I noticed him sprinkle some of his "breathe-easy" oil onto his handkerchief and then put it under his pillow. I suggested that it might be better to do that at night, because through the day, the oil would evaporate somewhat.

"No," he said. "It's just right by the time I go to bed."

I suggested then if he was doing it at night, he'd have to use less. But he simply became cross and emphatically declared, "Just get out of it! It's all right how it is. I know what I'm doing!"

"OK," I said. Under my breath, I continued, "I doubt very much that you do know what you are doing, but never mind!" That was a battle I wasn't prepared for, nor did I need to take it up.

After I'd done something for Geoffrey—turned on the oxygen, made him a cuppa, fixed something or sorted something—he'd rarely thank me or say anything. I didn't mind mostly, but some days when I'd felt as though I'd barely sat down, I'd say to him (sarcastically), "Thank you dear!"

Geoffrey would have no idea that I was being sarcastic, and he'd pipe up, "You're welcome," and he'd smile sweetly at me as if he had actually done something and I was genuinely thanking him.

23

I took Geoffrey into respite care on the morning I flew to Melbourne. I allowed plenty of time to get him settled, put his belongings away, ensure he knew where I was putting his things, where his room was, and how to get to the dining room and cafe. We had a coffee together at the cafe. As soon as his coffee arrived, he needed the bathroom. Fortunately, there were some right near the cafe, and I helped him towards them.

When he returned, he drank only half of his coffee and then said he'd had enough. We needed to take the lift back up to level 2, where his room was, but he had no idea where the lifts were. I pointed in the direction of the lifts, but he still could not see them. He could not see that the lifts were just past the planter boxes. He could only notice the planter boxes and didn't look beyond. That was another dementia thing: the inability to take in all of the surroundings. It was something I would forget about until Geoffrey was obviously lost within a space. Once back in his room, I said my goodbyes and promised I'd phone him the next day.

I left my car at home and took an Uber to the airport. I couldn't believe just how free I felt as soon as I was there. I felt slightly guilty at feeling so good, but I knew I desperately needed some serious time away from Geoffrey.

I collected my hired car at the Melbourne airport and had an easy drive to Tamara's place. It was *so* lovely to be there! I was still processing how easy it was travelling on my own and not having to accommodate

Geoffrey, sort him, organise him, guide him, help him, wait for him, and so on. I slept very well that night.

———————◆———————

The nine days in Melbourne flew by. I had a great time and especially enjoyed connecting again with friends and family, having fun lunches together, sharing good times over coffee, and having some great times with Tamara (and the beautiful Harvey-dog). It might sound awful, but I didn't miss Geoffrey. I phoned him every other day and kept the conversation light.

Usually he took a while to answer the phone, as it was on the opposite side of the bed from the chair in which he sat. He was usually quite breathless when he answered, and on each call, I gave him time to sit on his walker and catch his breath before he chatted. Not that he said much, but he did tell me that he attended some of concerts on a few afternoons. It was often difficult to understand him, as his speech was very broken because he was not only breathless but also struggled to find the words he needed.

When I returned to the Gold Coast, I went immediately to the meeting for carers held at Oz Care every second month. I was a little late, but it was wonderful to reconnect with the group, and the information from the mobility and disability products people was helpful. Then I had four whole days to myself before I picked Geoffrey up on the Tuesday morning. I made the most of them, allowing myself to have some rest, have some time in the pool, and do the chores at my leisure—delicious!

I weakened on the Sunday afternoon when I took the dogs in to visit Geoffrey. He was overjoyed to see me and the dogs. I stayed less than an hour, but that was about the limit he could cope with, and he was ready for a snooze when I left. I told him over and over that I'd pick him up at nine o'clock on Tuesday morning. He seemed happy with that. And it gave me the Monday to organise some things at home.

I took Missy to the vet to get her lumps checked, which were fine, and organised an air-conditioner service, as it was playing up. I had to post some parcels and make some important phone calls.

Tuesday morning arrived, and I wasn't sure how I felt. I had enjoyed my two weeks off immensely, and I wasn't sure if I could cope with Geoffrey after such a lovely break. I arrived to collect Geoffrey at nine in the morning. He wasn't ready for me and was sitting on the toilet when I went into his room. He had shoved his clothes into his suitcase—what a mess!

I put the suitcase on the bed and attempted to shuffle things around in order to get his other belongings into the case. There was almost a whole packet of pull-ups left over, and when I queried him about this, he grumped heartily at me. I stopped mid-step, looked him fair in the eye, and sharply told him that he needn't grump at me like that or I'd just leave him there instead of taking him home. *Good grief*, I thought, *not even five minutes in and he's already grumpy*. I felt my heart sink to my stomach.

One of the nurses put Geoffrey's socks and shoes on for him and helped me carry everything out to the car. The suitcase, oxygen converter, over-toilet chair, and wheelie-walker all had to be put into the car with us. As we approached the car, Geoffrey started to walk very wobbly on his own after leaving his walker at the back of the car.

I said, "Whoa! Use your walker all the way to the car door."

"I'm all right!" was his sharp retort.

He wasn't. It was a dangerous falls risk. Thankfully, the nurse was on my side, and the two of us insisted that he use the walker all the way to the passenger door of the car. I felt my heart sink to my stomach again. I sighed a big sigh, put the walker into the car, got in, and drove us home in silence. *Can I keep doing this?* I wondered to myself.

As we arrived home, Geoffrey apologised for grumping at me. I was a bit taken aback, as an apology was rare. Apology accepted. We moved on.

Unfortunately, it didn't take long to revisit sad again. Writing this made me cry. I was trapped again. I did not want to feel that way, but it took a lot of self-control to lift up my emotions.

The next day, one of the delightful care workers came to give Geoffrey his shower, and the morning began well. Very quickly, though, things deteriorated. Geoffrey couldn't explain something that he wanted to tell me about, and he became annoyed.

I had put his medication and supplements in front of him, and I'd made him a cup of tea, which I'd cooled slightly with some cold water and placed a straw into to make it easy for him to drink. I had forgotten to put a glass of water in front of him also, however, and he was complaining that his tea was too hot to take his pills with.

I was just finishing my breakfast, so I asked him to wait a couple of minutes until I finished, and I would get up and get some water. Despite the fact that he'd need to wait a couple of minutes, he continued to shove his pills into his mouth. I took a deep breath, ignored him, finished my breakfast, and then got him a glass of water.

"Oh, at last!" he wailed.

I said nothing, but I was feeling annoyed.

An hour and a half later, I had to leave for my Wednesday-morning commitment. Geoffrey usually would sit on his walker or his Luggie in the garage and wait for the bus to pick him up for his regular bus trip. I had prepared his Luggie by putting the straps of a bag over the back of the seat so that he had somewhere to put items he needed to take with him: a straw, spare hearing aid batteries, and his GTN spray in case of heart pain. I'd told him about putting the bag on his Luggie, but as we went to go out the door, he lunged towards my handbag on the hall table and asked if that was his bag. Before I'd had a chance to tell him no and remind him that his bag was already on the Luggie, he'd stepped in front of me and was totally blocking the way for me to either open the garage entry door or pick up my bag.

I was aware that I was cutting my time a bit fine; however, I waited till he began to move towards the garage entry door. Then I ducked past him, grabbed my bag, and opened the door for him. Of course, instead of stopping right at his Luggie and getting onto it, he kept walking and stopped right at the driver's door of the car, leaving me unable to get into the car. Plus, he was several steps past the Luggie.

He was unable to walk several steps without his walker, and when I attempted to tell him to go back next to his Luggie and just sit on it, he said huffily, "I'm all right."

But *I* wasn't all right. I couldn't get to the car, so I once again encouraged Geoffrey to move his walker back so that I could get into the car and he could get onto the Luggie. He did move but angrily said, "Oh, shut up" as he moved back towards the Luggie.

I don't know what happened inside of me, but I exploded. It was less than twenty-four hours since I'd picked him up, and I was full to the brim with sadness, anger, and fury. It was unfair. I was pissed off and blindly rageful. I swung my arm up and, as hard as I could, whacked him on the arm. "You bloody shut-up!" I yelled. "You are an ungrateful shit!"

I hate you, I thought to myself. *Why am I even doing this? What's the damn point?*

It took a while after I drove off for me to calm down. Why did I do this to myself? I knew I had to stop getting so angry. It wasn't doing either myself or Geoffrey any good. Lots of deep breaths and some loud music in the car, and I managed to regain some semblance of peace.

<hr />

The following day turned me around a great deal. I had booked in for a seminar day run by the Commonwealth Respite and Care-Link Services. It was being held at the Star (Casino) Gold Coast's Event Centre. A carer had been arranged for Geoffrey from 8.30 a.m. until 3 p.m. I wasn't sure what to expect, and although I was well used to doing things on my own, it still felt a bit weird.

Morning tea upon arrival meant that the participants had time to mingle and chat. I quickly introduced myself to a couple of other ladies who'd arrived at the same time as I did, and we spent a lovely twenty minutes or so discovering each other's stories. We were all caring for husbands with varying levels of dementia. We registered at the desk, went into the conference room, and sat at a table with three other ladies. Each table had beautiful flowers in the centre, glasses and cold-water jugs, bowls of yummy chocolates and sweets, as well as a nice little welcome gift of a couple of Lindt chocolate balls in a gauze bag and a card for each participant. Under each glass was a lucky door-prize ticket.

The speakers were interesting. First, a representative from My Aged Care talked about what My Aged Care was for, what it offered, and how to access it. The next speaker spoke about ten things we could do to keep our brains heathy. He was a very engaging speaker, and his presentation was interesting, heartening, and uplifting. He urged us not to try to do ten things at once or we would become overwhelmed and give up in a few weeks. His suggestion was to do one thing for at least a month before we introduced another. It was clear that unless carers looked after their own brain health, the stress and the constant nature of caring for someone would take its toll on us and our brains.

While the speakers were up front, there was a team of roving ladies giving each participant who wanted one a neck and shoulder massage. There was a half-hour break before lunch was ready, and everyone took that time to chat with the others at their table. I had my neck and shoulder massage in that break. Ooh, it was divine, and just what I needed. I was amazed to find how much more comfortable my neck and shoulders were after my massage. What a treat!

Five door prizes were given out, and two of the ladies at our table won prizes: lovely boxes of treats from the Body Shop.

Lunch was scrumptious: high-quality, plenty for everyone, great choices of main meals, and dessert and fruit available too. Over lunch, I chatted with one of the ladies I'd first met in the morning, and we had a nice connection and some laughs together.

We were presented with gifts from Commonwealth Respite and Care-link Services in a reusable carry bag. Then we were all given a meditation CD and a beautiful book. Wow, talk about feeling spoiled! It just felt like we were truly being appreciated and pampered.

The afternoon speakers were from the National Disability Insurance Scheme, and they were interesting and informative—not relevant to me, but I did discover some good gems of information I could pass on to Paul and Lyn, as they were applying for NDIS funding for Lyn.

Before we left, another five door prizes were called out. Another two ladies from our table won prizes, plus me. That meant that five out of six at our table won door prizes! We were the winning table for sure. There were twelve tables in total, with between six and eight people at each table, so we were amazed. It felt very special.

Then, as if we hadn't received enough, we were each given a Christmas gift bag from the Body Shop containing a couple of Body Shop goodies inside. Plus, a beautiful fresh flower, an iris, was given to each person on the way out.

I came home laden with all these gifts and feeling very uplifted. It was the whole package that made a difference: the day out; the fact that the day's program was well organised and run; the gifts; winning a door prize; the massage; chatting with women in the same situation as myself; the engaging speakers and the information they gave; the delicious food; and the validation given to us by everyone involved.

The first thing I chose to do for myself was to have a short meditation every day. It was something I hadn't done for ages, and I felt that I could do a mini meditation every day at a time when Geoffrey was not going to interrupt me. I managed to do it the first week, about five days out of the seven. I didn't stress or beat myself up for the missed days. So far, so good, I thought instead, and I decided that if I could continue with five days a week, every week, I'd be heaps better off than I had been.

24

It was November 2018, and Geoffrey was deteriorating in every way. He was breathless more often, his memory was worse, he was finding it difficult to talk, and when he did, I often couldn't understand what he was talking about because he missed words or used the wrong words here and there.

He had never been a fast talker, but by mid-November, I had to be very, very patient indeed, because it would take him a very long time to get his words out. There were lots of ahs and ums and much repeating of the same words over and over before we got the next word. It was a painfully slow process. I would attempt to guess the words he was trying to get out and usually that worked fairly well, but at other times it was impossible.

I knew he was frustrated with himself, and I did my best to make it as easy as possible by anticipating his needs whenever I could. He was walking much slower and having to stop and rest every five to ten metres. I found that I had to cut up his meat for him, as he was no longer able to do it. He struggled to coordinate his knife and fork, and I did my best to prepare meals he could just use a spoon for. He also announced one morning that he didn't want boiled eggs for breakfast anymore. Eventually I worked out that it was because he found it too difficult to wrestle with the shells and get the egg out.

Geoffrey had an appointment with the cardiologist, who had been doing his best to get Geoffrey referred to one of the large hospitals in Brisbane in order to have a procedure done which could stop the leak around his replaced aortic valve. Up until then, it had come to nothing. That day, when the cardiologist listened to Geoffrey's heart, it was noticeably worse than the previous visit, so he called upon another specialist whom he knew as a friend as well as a colleague.

The cardiologist told us that if we didn't receive communication about the procedure within three weeks, we were to get back in touch with him. In the meantime, we were to get Geoffrey to University Hospital should his breathing deteriorate so that if Geoffrey lay flat, his breathing was worse. Then we were to give them the cardiologist's card and say that Geoffrey was one of his patients. As Geoffrey got into the car after the appointment, he said that he hoped the procedure could be done soon, because he didn't think he could keep going much longer like he was. I felt sad for him.

The very next afternoon, Geoffrey lost the majority of sight in his right eye. He was rattled and became very anxious. He'd had times where he'd felt giddy and had told me that he had double vision. These episodes usually lasted a half hour at most. This loss of sight persisted, so I fed the dogs early and took him to the emergency department of University Hospital in Southport. He also had to have his GTN spray for heart pain twice through the day, plus another time on the way to the hospital.

Although the emergency department was very busy, it wasn't long before he was taken in to a bed. A number of doctors examined him and asked us many questions over and over. Eventually, after a number of blood tests, an X-ray, and a CAT scan, they admitted him to the medical assessment unit. It was very late before he was seen by the unit's doctor. I eventually left him at 1.30 a.m., and I got to bed at 2 a.m. To say that I was tired would have been an understatement.

I was up early in order to be back at the hospital by nine so that I could be there when the senior doctor saw him. Although the doctors had their suspicions, they wanted Geoffrey to see the ophthalmologist at the clinic that afternoon. He had a one o'clock appointment. Before his lunch came, I shoved him over on his bed and lay down with him snuggled into my back, and I had a nap for about forty-five minutes. It was delicious! I so needed the sleep, and Geoffrey enjoyed cuddling me.

At the appropriate time, a wheelchair appeared with a lovely lady who wheeled Geoffrey up to the clinic. I was very glad she knew where to go and how to get there, because I would have had no idea at all. The hospital was very large, and the clinic section was big also.

We arrived at the correct place, and we waited and waited. What followed was a series of tests, waiting some more, seeing eye doctors, and waiting before more tests and more doctors. We finished there just before five o'clock. It was exhausting for both of us.

The senior ophthalmologist ordered a series of blood tests which hadn't been done yet during this admission, and he wanted the results of two of them to be received back before it could be decided if Geoffrey could go home. The concern was that Geoffrey might have some inflammation of the nerve to the eye.

At 6.30 p.m., my next-door neighbour phoned me to see if everything was OK because our dogs had been barking until late the night before, and they had started barking again that afternoon. I told him that Geoffrey was in hospital and that I had been there until very late the night before, and that I should be home by about 8.30 p.m.

He wanted to know if there was anything he could do for us, and he wished Geoffrey well.

Thank goodness our neighbours were lovely and understanding. I knew I needed to ensure someone else had a key to our house so that if I had to take Geoffrey to the hospital another time, someone could go and get the dogs or, at the very least, spend some time with them. The dogs were not used to being alone for such long periods, and Missy in particular suffered a bit of separation anxiety.

At 8.30 p.m., we headed home. The diagnosis was that Geoffrey had had a mini-stroke behind his right eye. Nothing could be done about that. He was on aspirin, which was as much anticoagulant as he could take because of his past history of bowel bleeding.

The other thing they suspected—because of the blood results, weight loss, and other symptoms—was polyps in the bowel which were a little inflamed, or he might have malignant tumours in the bowel. Either way, they wouldn't investigate that any further because even if they found something, his heart condition meant he wouldn't survive a general anaesthetic for surgery to fix it. So, in essence, nothing could be done about any bowel problems. He was a bit confused about it all, and he was just happy to get home.

Amazingly, I felt OK about it all. It was how it was, and I could do nothing to change it, so getting upset would help nothing and no one. I was tired, weary, and a bit unmotivated to do a lot, but I felt fine about Geoffrey. I let family and friends know what was going on in the most honest way I could. I still felt fine. I did wonder if I was just working over the top of other feelings, but it didn't feel that way. I was truly OK with the situation.

There was plenty I could have worried about if I'd wanted to: What would I do when Geoffrey died? What would I do for money? How would I manage? How was I going to manage the house, the garden, the maintenance, and the bills? Would it be best to just sell the house and rent something until the apartment was ready? And much more! I just didn't feel that it mattered.

I was OK at that time, and I was managing OK, so there was no point in worrying. I knew that Geoffrey could die at any time, and I was still OK. In some ways, I knew that part of me would be relieved when he passed, because he was a lot of work.

Another part of me wanted to feel guilty about that. In all honesty, though, it would be a relief. It didn't mean that I loved him any less, only that I'd be free to live the next part of my life, whatever that was going to look like. In a way, it was no different than when I really enjoyed my respite times. I knew that it was perfectly all right for me to have time off, and it was important that I have that time off in order to recharge my own batteries.

Inside myself, I knew that I would make the right decisions when the time came, and that I'd be all right. In the meantime, it was a day-to-day thing, and I did what needed to be done day by day.

The deterioration was very slow and sometimes almost unnoticeable. There were some days when Geoffrey was still fairly good cognitively, but other days he'd tie me up in knots and do my head in. He'd call me to say that he wanted the oxygen on, then just as I was starting on cleaning the floor tiles, he'd call again and say he needed help because he couldn't get the music to play on the "stupid computer". He had opened a YouTube page and was clicking everything in sight to get it to play the music. I took one look at the screen; everything looked normal. I could faintly hear music playing, so in the first instant, I was puzzled.

pool shop to purchase some pool supplies. By the time I did get home, I was somewhere near normal. Thank God for the beach!

I had ignored the pool maintenance for a while, so it took a few days for me get it back in a stable condition. It was a process to add the acid, the add the salt and all the other stabilising chemicals that the pool needed. It was good, though, to be working outside. I found once again that the fresh air and sunshine helped me to keep my mood up.

I knew I needed to use the pool regularly, as I did find it meditative and peaceful. The trick was to ensure that Geoffrey was set up to be OK for a while; otherwise, after me being in the pool for barely five minutes, he would call out to me and ask if I was going to be much longer. I'd feel under pressure to get out and attend to whatever it was that he wanted/needed. I needed at *least* half an hour in the pool for it to work its magic on me.

I needed the meditative effect of the pool because I was growing increasingly anxious. The thing that made it worse was if I watched the news. I couldn't emotionally cope with the barrage of bad news items: murders, another killer gets two life sentences, a schoolie falling from an eleventh-floor balcony, worrying international relations, protests, and so on. It all just made me feel physically sick and increased my general anxiety.

Geoffrey wanted to watch several news reports on TV every day. I had to ensure that the sound was muted (he could hear it directly through his hearing aids) and that I had something else to do so that I didn't even glance at the screen. In the past, I had not had such extreme reactions, but I felt quite vulnerable. Contrary to usual, I felt very sensitive and emotionally reactive.

The first Saturday of December, our friends John and Trina came from the Sunshine Coast to visit for the day. It was also close to a big birthday for Lyn, and so she and Paul came over to join us for lunch. We had a lovely day, and Geoffrey was fairly good while everyone was there. Afterwards, he was pretty knocked out, and he slept a lot. I know that he enjoyed seeing John again, as they hadn't seen each other in a long time.

Geoffrey was fairly washed out, weary, and confused for the next several days. It was very hard to have a conversation with him. He couldn't explain what he meant when he'd said something that didn't make sense. He knew he couldn't find the words, and often he would forget what he'd wanted to say before he found the words to complete the sentence. It was frustrating for both of us.

In so many ways, he was just like a big child. I knew that was the way with dementia, but it was the inconsistency of it that surprised me almost every time. He didn't act like a child with everything; it would just regularly occur here and there. Also, I felt increasingly lonely because of the lack of communication. If I was on my own, it felt as though it would be better or easier, because there would be no one there to whom I might expect to talk with. Geoffrey was there, but he was progressively more and more uncommunicative.

At the same time, he was growing more and more dependent without even realising all that I needed to do for him:

- get his clothes out for him
- put his pull-ups on or take them off and dispose of them
- put in his hearing aids
- help him shave or finish off his shave for him
- empty his urine-bottle each morning from beside the bed
- make his meals and snacks and drinks
- put his adult bib on and off

- cut up his meat
- get his medications and supplements for him
- ensure that he had a straw for his drinks
- clear his plates and glasses and cups away
- make sure he had his GTN spray with him no matter where he went
- take his donut pillow from the wheelchair to his armchair or vice versa
- turn the oxygen converter on or off over and over
- help him with the computer
- turn the fan on or off
- help him get into bed sometimes
- flush the toilet when he'd forgotten
- clean up toilet messes

and more, so much more. Often, I'd just need extra patience in order to wait for him to do things like:

- get out of the way
- get out of a doorway
- go to the toilet before we went out
- sort some imaginary thing before he moved or started to head out the door
- fiddle with his hearing aids
- mute the TV so I could ask him something
- find the words to say what he wanted to say

All these were minor in themselves, but they added to the extra things he'd call me for (and he needed to ask for these things).

On top of all that was the general running of the household: emptying bins; cleaning; paying bills and keeping the finances in order;

making medical and allied health appointments for Geoffrey; looking after the mail and the pool; and in general, just keeping an eye and an ear on him so that he was safe or I could anticipate his needs.

Overall, though, the most stressful times were those in which Geoffrey would attempt to do things he was not physically able to do by himself, and he actually needed to just ask me for help or to get him something. I never knew when this might occur, because usually, he'd just call me or ask me for what he needed. One time, he had disappeared for a while, and I thought he'd gone to the toilet, but he emerged with his shorts off and his old jeans in his hands. He called out, "Where you to?" (meaning *where have you gone to?*). As it happened, I was right beside him sitting on a chair, but with his eye problem and his lack of awareness, he hadn't seen me.

It turned out that he was cold, so he had taken off his shorts and looked for some long pants. His old jeans were way too big for him, because he had lost over eighteen kilos since he had last worn them. I had no idea how he'd found them, because I thought I had well and truly buried all his too-big clothes in the back of his wardrobe. I took the old jeans from him and told him that those jeans were going to be way too big for him. He mumbled something about those being the only long pants he had.

I took the jeans back to the bedroom wardrobe, put them up on a high shelf, and grabbed a pair of trackpants for him. I straightened out all the shelves that he had rummaged through in order to find some pants. His shorts had been dropped on the bedroom floor, so I emptied the pockets and put the shorts into the wash-basket. I went back down to the family room and sat Geoffrey down, took off his sandals, helped him on with the trackpants, and put his sandals back on him.

Another time, he thought he'd turn on the oxygen by himself rather than ask me to do it. He managed to become dangerously tangled in the hose. By the time he called to me, I was in the laundry and totally unaware that he had gone to do this. He just called out, "Where you to?" I didn't realise he needed anything, and I thought he was just worried because he couldn't see where I was, which was a common thing.

I called out that I was in the laundry, thinking that was it. He didn't reply and gave me no indication that he needed assistance, so I took my time and finished what I was doing. When I surfaced, I quickly saw that he was in a very tangled and precarious position in the lounge room, and he hadn't let me know he needed help.

I dashed over and untangled him. I had no idea how he had managed to get so tangled in the oxygen hose. I helped him rebalance and got him back to his chair. I put the oxygen prongs in place for him, went back to the lounge, and turned on the oxygen.

These examples in themselves don't sound like much, but multiply it by many different incidents, and it becomes stressful and tiring. I was constantly exhausted.

25

" I feel funny," stated Geoffrey one evening.

"OK," I said. "Funny in what way?" It took him ages to give me an answer, and while he was searching for words, I said, "Oh yes, you have been hilarious today. Is that it? Is that the funny?"

He laughed a little, and it lightened up the pressure on him, but he was still unable to tell me what "I feel funny" meant. He had no pain, and his blood pressure was OK, but his oxygen saturation was a little low at 90 per cent, so I got the oxygen for him in the hope that it would help. What else could I do? It was frustrating when he couldn't exactly tell me what was going on. I did feel that often I was only guessing as to what he needed. Then I'd hope there wouldn't be any repercussions.

Geoffrey was becoming increasingly vague with his communication. I did a lot of guessing! There was not a lot of communication regarding the television either. Often, about three quarters of the way through a program, perhaps an interesting documentary, he would suddenly grab the remote control and would change the channel. Annoyingly, it was often when I was engrossed in the program.

"Oi!" I'd exclaim. "What are you doing? Don't change the channel now please."

Sometimes he just said that he didn't know what he was doing, and I would change the TV back to the channel we were watching. Sometimes if I said that the program wasn't finished, he'd say haltingly, "Oh, didn't know. Thought finished."

Most mornings when he woke, he'd ask me what day it was. The conversation went something like this: "What time is the woman coming?"

"What woman?" I'd ask.

"Shower," he'd respond.

I'd follow with, "There's no one coming today, darling."

Geoffrey would say, "But it's Monday, isn't it?"

"No honey, it's Tuesday today."

"Oh yeah, I thought Tuesday!" was his reply. Other times it was, "It's Monday today, isn't it?" and when I told him that it was Tuesday, he said, "Thought so!"

He wasn't remembering the care workers' names now, even our regular people. He was also struggling a little with names of family members. He slept of lot of each day.

———◆◆◆———

On Sunday, we had breakfast out, and then I asked him if he wanted to go for a drive. He eagerly said yes. Taking a drive around was something I knew he used to enjoy. I drove towards the coast. We cruised around Chevron Island, and he commented on some of the houses. We drove through Surfers Paradise and along the Esplanade. The sea was a beautiful blue, and the waves were crashing savagely on the shore, but it was pretty.

We drove up past Sea World and along the Spit. Geoffrey enjoyed seeing all the boats and all the people having picnics and fun on the shore of the Broadwater. I turned around, taking the scenic route in the general direction of home, and as we returned through Surfers Paradise, I noticed he was flagging. I suggested we head straight home, as he looked weary.

He thought about it a bit and then agreed that he was a bit weary. Once we were home, he slept the majority of the rest of the day. He had enjoyed the drive, but it clean tuckered him out.

———————— ·◆· ————————

That week, he seemed extra weary, and he seemed to be needing the oxygen rather a lot. On the Tuesday morning, he had a fall. He had been in the bathroom and instead of taking his wheelie-walker right up to where he wanted to be (which was something I had been nagging him about for ages, because it was so dangerous when he lurched across to grab a bench or whatever was close), he parked it next to the shower, and he wasn't close enough to the vanity to hold on to it and gain his balance. Down he went on the hard tiles.

He said he was OK and dismissed my idea of calling an ambulance. I managed to help him to turn over and get onto his knees, and I helped pull him up while he used the wheelie-walker to pull himself up too. Phew!

It didn't seem as though anything was broken, but about an hour later, he was complaining that his bottom and coccyx area was sore. He had an extra sore bottom for a number of days. I wasn't surprised. I was more surprised that he didn't seem to have done any other damage.

There was no preventing Geoffrey from having falls like this, because no matter how often I pointed out that he needed to take his walker right up to where he was wanting to go, he insisted, and I mean *really* insisted, that he was OK and didn't need to do that. He could reach!

He slept the whole morning in the chair, and by the afternoon, we were very grateful that we had purchased a donut cushion for his chair, because he really needed it. His bottom was indeed very sore! He snoozed off in the chair after lunch, suddenly woke, pulled himself to his feet leaning on the walker, took a few steps into the room, and stood there. I asked him where he was going. He looked at me with a puzzled look and said that he didn't know. I asked if he needed to go to the toilet, and he said no. He returned to his chair for about five minutes, then he got up again and took himself to the toilet.

He would be snoozing in the chair and he'd wake up, look over at me, and ask me something totally unintelligible. When I questioned him gently about what he wanted, I got more unintelligible mumble and the occasional random word. I smiled and said that I didn't understand what he wanted. He'd pause, look around, and say that he didn't know either. Then he would go back to sleep.

The overwhelmed feeling was intermingled with feeling sad, very sad. I seemed unable to shake it. Although Geoffrey was weak, wobbly, and sometimes incoherent, he looked well. He had good colour and just looked well and healthy. It was weird. He looked like he could live for years yet, and that made me feel completely trapped. I knew I couldn't manage this for years more.

I spoke to our financial advisor to see what options I had. It appeared that it was going to be a very expensive exercise if Geoffrey went into full-time care. I had a small amount of money put aside in an investment account, but ... oh-oh, there I was, feeling overwhelmed again! Putting Geoffrey into care was clearly off the table. It was way too costly. I probably should have gone to Centrelink to get the real information, but at that time, it just seemed too much. Going into Centrelink always involved a long wait.

Talking about costs, I finally managed to pay someone to paint the exterior of the house. It only took a few days, but it was so lovely to have it done before Christmas. I was quite proud of myself that I had managed to save enough money in order to have it done. Apart from the damaged garage door, the house now looked lovely again.

———————◆———————

Before Christmas 2018, my son, Mick; his wife and their son, came for a visit. The next day, Tamara arrived with her dog, then Fiona arrived with her dog. It was to be the first Christmas we'd had together for years.

After Christmas, Mick and his family would go home, and then Fiona's dog would be picked up and her children were arriving and would spend my and my grandson's birthday plus the new year with us. Although it was lovely to have my three kids with me, there were some family tensions, and I found that I was not emotionally able to cope very well at all. I was in tears at every little thing. I felt sad inside. I was anxious all the time. My stomach churned, and I cried again and again.

Even though it was good to have everyone help in various ways with Geoffrey, I felt like I was constantly on edge. Any raised voice or slightly critical tone, and I was an emotional wreck, even if it was just Fiona getting a bit cross with her children over something. I felt physically sick at the thought of wishing anyone Merry Christmas. I didn't seem to be able to get myself anywhere near balanced or peaceful no matter what internal work I did.

ABC didn't work. Asking myself over and over the question *What benefit am I getting out of feeling bad?* did nothing. I tried every single technique in the toolbox, but my sad sick stomach churned more and my eyes continued to leak.

The birthdays arrived. It was my sixty-fourth and my grandson's eighth. First thing in the morning, he became upset because he had wanted to write my name in their birthday card to me and not just on the envelope. He cracked a wobbly, and Fiona was cross with him. I was a mess. It was not a good way to start my birthday, but I felt sad and stomach-churningly emotionally fragile.

I looked at Geoffrey snoozing in the chair. He had been a combination of very with it and very confused each day. He was sleeping a great deal, still losing weight, and very fussy with what he wanted to eat. I never knew what was coming next with him. It didn't ease my tension.

I managed to put on my plastic-fantastic face, and we went out for lunch. Lyn and Paul joined us, and a young man I'd become friends with from the cafe made us a birthday cake and also joined us for lunch. It was pleasant, and my anxiety momentarily eased ever so slightly. Geoffrey managed the lunch very well, but he didn't talk much.

I had a huge number of messages on Facebook, texts, and some phone calls to wish me a happy birthday. Almost every one of them made me cry. The only phone call I took was when Mick phoned in the evening; the others I let go to my message bank because I was not in a state to be able to take so many birthday wishes, nor was I able to hold it together in order to talk much. I did not want people's sympathy. I certainly didn't need anyone trying to help with advice, because I felt like I'd tried everything. I was taking vitamin and mineral supplements as well as antidepressants, and I still felt overwhelmed and hopeless.

───◆•◉•◆───

On New Year's Day, Erin called via video messenger to show us the fireworks in Prague (where they were holidaying). It was a short call, but Geoffrey was very impressed. He marvelled at the technology that enable such great communication. It was nice to see a smile on his face.

The next day, Tamara and Fiona took the children to the movies. Geoffrey went on his bus trip, and I had a day off from everyone and everything. I really needed the time and space. I managed to calm my insides a little, and I did feel a bit better.

By the time Fiona and the children went home, I was beginning to feel slightly less anxious, and my insides felt a little more unwound than before. The deep sadness was still there, and tears could still well up quickly depending upon what was going on at the time. It still didn't take much for my eyes to leak again.

As soon as Fiona and the children went home, even though Tamara was still with us for another three days, Geoffrey returned to his usual behaviour. He was rude, inconsiderate, thoughtless, demanding, and grumpy. I was beyond frustrated with him.

On an intellectual level, I totally understood that he no longer had the brain capacity to be anything else. He had the comprehension, consideration, and care and appreciation of nothing more than a toddler. Emotionally, though, I hated him.

Don't get me wrong: I loved Geoffrey, the man I knew and loved. This was no longer him, and I well and truly and utterly hated who and how he was. I wanted to rant and complain at him, but it was a total waste of energy. I wanted to physically hit him, but violence got me nowhere. I wanted to inflict hurtful words and get revenge on him, but he wouldn't even understand. Part of me felt downright gutted that I just had to put up with his shit.

———◆———

Before Tamara went home, she cooked up a huge amount of delicious chicken and vegetable lasagne. We had some for dinner, and we packaged up the rest in serving-size pieces and put them in the freezer. I was extremely grateful to have some scrumptious instant meals for the coming weeks.

After Tamara left, Geoffrey looked at me and said, "I suppose I'll have to talk more now!"

"No," I said to him. "You needn't bother."

You cunning devil, I thought. He knew to pull his head in a bit when everyone was there.

There was little interaction between us other than what was absolutely necessary. After a couple of days, my compassion returned slightly. But there still wasn't any conversation.

I felt as if I really wasn't cut out for this dementia journey. I had never been a people-pleaser. I had always been outspoken, an independent thinker, a teacher, and a leader. I was not made to be subservient or quiet.

I fully understood that in order to do this journey of Geoffrey's dementia easily, I needed to shut up and not react to his nonsense. I needed to be acquiescent, yielding, and agreeable all the time. Who I was, was actually the total opposite. I could do this for only short spaces of time. I knew full well that I was often making things harder for myself because of this, but I also knew that it was against my true nature to be that compliant continually on an ongoing basis.

Paul came over to fix a leaky toilet for me. As Paul was inspecting the problem and I was listening to him about what tools he would need, I turned around and found Geoffrey right behind me. I couldn't get past him. I asked him to back up and move out of the way, but he just moved to the main hallway and blocked my way again.

I managed to get around him and went via the lounge and dining room towards a drawer in the family room to collect a screwdriver. I asked Geoffrey (nicely) if he could move out of the walkway. He just moved sideways, and in doing so, scraped the wall of the passage with the wheels of his walker.

Oh my God, I thought, *it will cost me a fortune to get all these scrape marks fixed when I sell the house!* I still couldn't get past him so I moved Geoffrey back towards the middle of the walkway. I told him that his wheels were scraping the wall.

"It's OK," he snapped.

I said that I still couldn't get past him.

"Yes, you can!" he quickly retorted.

"I wouldn't ask you to move if I could get past you," I replied.

"Yes, you would!" was his comeback.

I just sighed.

Then Paul came around the corner, and it was obvious to a blind man that Geoffrey was in the way. Eventually, as Paul and I waited in front of him, he moved.

"Would you like a cup of tea?" I asked Geoffrey.

"No," he said.

So I only made myself and Paul a cuppa.

As I sat down with it, Geoffrey moaned at me, "What about me? Where is mine?"

I reminded him that he had said he didn't want one.

"No, I didn't. You didn't even ask me!" he bellowed crossly.

It was mildly frustrating, to say the least.

I know I have mentioned this before in this narrative, but if I was to multiply this scenario by about twenty times, that would be the average number of times this type of thing would happen in the average week. If I gave him a choice of two things, he'd choose one, then say I was wrong when I served it up because he'd chosen the other. If I didn't give him a choice, he'd complain about not being given a choice. It went on and on.

I was most definitely a little bit better emotionally than I had been over the Christmas period, but I still had a deep sadness underneath my everyday ability to look and sound normal. I still found myself fighting tears every day. I would receive a beautiful text from someone in Melbourne expressing love and support or sending me a virtual hug, and I couldn't read the message without crying. If someone gave me an actual hug, I couldn't speak for the lump in my throat.

I added a B vitamin capsule to my daily supplement intake, hoping that might help. I thought that it would probably take a while. In the meantime, I felt like every minute of every day was a struggle. I was miserable, and I just couldn't seem to pull myself out of it.

Geoffrey had no idea that I was unhappy. He just plodded along as usual. I think that he didn't even realise that he was rude or grumpy towards me much of the time. He thought that life was fine. He would occasionally become annoyed that he couldn't do certain things, but mostly he thought that I was just being bossy when I would not let him attempt to do some things.

26

In early January, we received notification from Prince Charles Hospital in Brisbane that Geoffrey had to come and have a transoesophageal echocardiogram at the end of the month. This was a scan taken from down his oesophagus and involved a mild anaesthetic. It was needed so that the doctors could get a better picture of his heart, with a view to being able to see if fixing his regurgitating mitral valve might be possible.

The hospital was a full hour and a half away, and the letter said that he had to be there by 8 a.m., which probably meant a two-hour drive in morning traffic. I was not looking forward to that. Big drive, big day!

Part of me saw that this appointment was a good thing. The other part of me—the overwhelmed, trapped person—was devastated that if his heart could be repaired, it just meant that my imprisoning circumstances would go on forever. Not very nice of me, I know, but to be honest, the only way I could see out of this nightmare was when Geoffrey died. This made me judge myself to be a total bitch.

It felt like I was either being horrible or more horrible, and this left me even more sad and overwhelmed. What an awful cycle to be in. With no apparent way out, I was stumped as to how to feel better. I was hitting the bottom of the barrel again, and I felt awful.

I managed, over a couple of days, to have conversations with some of my soul family members and just being able to be 100 per cent honest and real in order to have a good rant and let it all out did help.

It resolved some of the overwhelmed feelings. However, the sadness remained.

My lovely GP let me have another good rant, and again, it helped. She also gave me a new referral to see the psychologist that I'd seen previously for PTSD. I couldn't get an appointment for about a month, though, so I just had to deal with things myself until then.

For some reason, or no reason at all, Geoffrey began to be nice to me again. He told me that he loved me. He thanked me for many of the things I did each day for him. He voiced his appreciation on a number of occasions, and he just seemed happier within himself. I found this to be a pleasant change, and it helped to alleviate some of the sadness. But I still felt trapped.

The weeks passed, and I was eventually able to sort out the mess regarding the damaged garage door. It took several phone calls and then another one-hour call to the insurance company. The following day, the insurance company paid, and I was able to arrange to get the garage door replaced. At last!

Emotionally, I was taking things one day at a time. Just because Geoffrey was being more pleasant for the most part didn't mean that he remembered to flush the toilet. Neither did he realise when he'd made a mess somewhere. Nor did he remember that he'd asked the same question over and over, and so essentially, all of the usual dementia stuff went on.

Geoffrey was using oxygen most days. Some days, he tested his oxygen saturation dozens of times, like he was obsessed. Other days, he would only check it a couple of times. His blood pressure was under control thanks to his medications, but he still checked it at least twice a day.

Because physically Geoffrey was feeling a bit better and was able to eat more things now that his lower dentures were fitting well, he took more risks physically. He was not stable on his feet, but because he had a bit more energy, he thought he could leave his wheelie-walker and just use two sticks. Wrong! He was *so* wobbly. It was very dangerous for him, but he kept insisting that he was doing OK. Oh my God, it was infuriating, and he would not listen to me at all. I remember thinking that I should hide those blasted sticks.

———◆———

As I have mentioned earlier, on Wednesdays Geoffrey went on the bus trip with Liberty Community Connect. This enabled me to work on Wednesday mornings plus have an hour or so to myself. I use the word *work* lightly here, because what I did never seemed like work to me.

I am a clairvoyant, and I have connected with people who have passed over. I have seen various things, heard things, felt things, and known things since I was a small child. I'm able to turn this on or off these days, depending upon if I am working or not. I have not mentioned this earlier in this narrative because I didn't want it to be the focus of this book. In essence, in my life, I am just the same as everyone else. I very rarely receive information for myself or my family, but when strangers come to me, I can tell them an enormous amount about themselves and their past, present, and future—as well as information about and for their family and close friends.

Wednesday mornings were always the best part of the week for me. There was a fabulous cafe in Worongary, Le Vintage Boutique Cafe, only ten minutes from home. They took the bookings for me, and I just turned up and did half-hour readings for however many people had booked in. Sometimes it was one person; sometimes it was up to six clients in a morning.

I'd sit in their beautiful garden. The staff were wonderful, and the ambiance of the cafe was the best I've ever come across. It was the perfect place for me to work. I had shade and misting fans when it was hot. They made me a coffee each week, and I got to chat with a great many lovely people and help them.

There was no advertising except for a flyer on the front counter and a mention on their Facebook page initially, so the great majority of my clients came from word-of-mouth referrals. It was a privilege to work there, and it always lifted my heart, no matter how awful I'd been feeling. I think in some way it saved my sanity, as some weeks I'd just manage a day at a time continually looking forward to my lovely refreshing Wednesday mornings. I loved my art class morning too, but it was different. On Wednesdays I was able to create peace of mind and unexpected, primarily happy contributions for other people, which was rewarding and peaceable for me.

I was always a bit backwards in coming forward with regard to my work. I would tend to not necessarily tell people unless I was directly asked what I did or if the topic came up some other way. Geoffrey, on the other hand, would tell all and sundry that he was proud of me and my abilities. He would boast that I was the best in Australia. It was vaguely embarrassing, but there was no way I was going to be able to stop him from just blabbing it to everyone.

Although I am confident in the fact that what I do is very real, and I use my abilities to help people, and I do help create positive changes in people's lives, I am well aware that not everyone believes in this stuff. Some people believe that it is positively evil. That's why I usually wait until I know someone a bit better before I mention it. I have often felt a bit sorry for the people Geoffrey told all this to.

Any of our new care workers usually got it from him on their very first service. Occasionally, this resulted in people coming to see me at the cafe.

———————◆———————

The afternoon before Geoffrey's hospital test procedure, I received a phone call from one of the nurses at the hospital in Brisbane asking me to fill them in on some more health information about Geoffrey. She reassured me not to worry if we were late, because she could see where we were coming from.

About two hours later, I received another call from the hospital, this time from one of the doctors. She asked me more about Geoffrey's medical history and about his level of dementia. That was hard. How would I put a level on it? He was perfectly OK in some ways but very not OK in others.

He was certainly more with-it than dementia patients in residential care. Geoffrey knew what was happening each day, even if he sometimes had to ask a couple of times. He could take himself to the toilet, even though he also needed pull-ups because he often didn't quite make it to the toilet in time. He could feed himself, even though I often had to cut up his food and he made a mess while eating. He forgot people's names, but he knew his family.

I did my best to be honest with the doctor's questions. She said that the referring local cardiologist had not included anything about Geoffrey's vascular dementia or other medical history, and she had concerns regarding his cognitive function possibly being further impaired by the anaesthetic for the test. She suggested that the test the next day be cancelled for now and that Geoffrey might need to see their cardiologist and possibly their geriatrician before going ahead with the test.

It was also a consideration that even if the test went well, the actual procedure of a repair of one of his leaking heart valves might be too risky. She stressed that even though the surgery was via the femoral artery and wasn't open-heart surgery, it was still a fairly major procedure and might in itself be too risky. She intended to contact our GP and the local cardiologist, as well as have a chat with their cardiologist. She said that she would call me back within the next couple of days with a decision about how to proceed. We were off the hook for the big drive to northern Brisbane for now.

The way it was talked about on the phone made me a little nervous about letting them muck about with Geoffrey's heart at all. If there was a fair chance that his cognitive function could decline further, I wasn't happy with that as an outcome, especially if the surgery was going to extend his life. The cost might be a bit high.

I left a message with the Blue Care schedulers and asked very hopefully if Geoffrey's Thursday service could be reinstated for the next day. Thankfully, all was OK, and a care worker came the next day as usual.

The following week, we had appointments with our GP. She basically agreed that the whole heart thing was very risky. After much discussion and many questions, we decided to say no to the investigation procedure. In doing so, we were also saying no to the possible fix of one of his leaky heart valves. A tough decision made!

———◦•◦•◦———

I was feeling a bit lonely. Having a proper conversation or discussion with Geoffrey was becoming harder. Even though I'd had a few phone conversations and Facebook video chats with my beautiful Melbourne soul-family members, I felt as if I hadn't really made proper friends here on the coast.

The universe gave me the answer quick smart! Within two days, I bumped into five people I knew who all wanted to stop and chat. Some reminded me to call so we could have coffee together or something. *OK, thank you, universe*, I thought.

It was up to me to keep some of these connections moving. OK, I got it! I had to be proactive in keeping up and creating greater friendships. Just a reminder that I was the creator of my life.

INSIGHT - FIFTEEN

Every action has an equal and opposite reaction. What this means in our life is that whatever we put out or do or think will return to us. If something goes one way, the reaction will come back another way to us. What we choose and how we choose also returns to us in some way.

In reality, we have infinite choices—although sometimes, it doesn't feel like it! We have infinite choices in what to think, how to feel, and actions/reactions/responses to take. In caring for a loved one, what we can forget is that the first choice we made was to care for the person we look after. After that, there are always choices about how we feel with each and every challenge that comes along. These challenges include making the choice to continue to look after our loved one.

In feeling trapped, or feeling as though we have no choices day to day, we are not necessarily enjoying life. This is how it has been for me at times, and if this is you too, then consider where you can make better choices to be happier. It really is a choice.

Make the choice to give yourself some time off so that you can hold on to your compassion and caring. Make the choice to care with love. And make the choice to love yourself as well in the process. Consciously choosing is empowering and helps to lower levels of frustration because you are making the choice or choices.

One evening just after dinner, Geoffrey got up from his comfy chair and leant down to grab the hose from his oxygen machine. He was just pulling at it, and when I asked him what he was doing and did he need the oxygen, I received a gruff mumble as a reply. I worked out that he didn't need the oxygen but was trying to pull or straighten out or do something with the hose itself. I had no idea why or what was going on in his head.

He had let go of his walker and, in doing so, had wobbled dangerously, moving sideways and away from his walker, all the while pulling on the oxygen hose. His lack of balance was scary; he could easily have fallen hard on the tiles. When I tried to stop him or get him to use his walker—or *shock! horror!* actually tell me what he needed so that I could do it for him—he became really snappy.

I said in a firm voice, "Stop! Stop! Geoffrey, stop!"

He snapped in a whining voice, "Why?"

I quickly came in and said, "Because what you are doing is dangerous. You are unbalanced and could fall."

"Why?" he quickly wailed again.

"You are being stupid and stubborn," I said. "If you fall and hurt yourself, you'll end up in hospital and then in care. You won't be able to come home."

"No, I'm not," he retorted.

Oh my God, I thought. *He is acting like a 3-year old. He's wailing and whining like a 3-year old—no logic, no awareness, no ability to be logical.*

I said nothing else, and he eventually wobbled back to his chair and sat down.

I got up and took myself into the dining room, where I worked on my craft project. I just couldn't bear to sit there right next to him any longer. I had to physically remove myself and focus on something else. I felt as though I was saving my sanity.

After a while, Geoffrey came in to the dining room and apologised for being stubborn. I told him that I was struggling to cope when he turned into a 3-year-old having a tantrum and being irresponsible. What followed almost resembled a normal conversation. He expressed his need to have a go at doing some things. He was frustrated at not being able to do much.

Regardless of the risks, I agreed to let him have a go at more things, even if it looked dangerous to me. I knew I would have to zipper my lip and just let him go. If he fell, he fell. I knew I'd been there before, but he had deteriorated over the past six months, and it was even more dangerous when he tried to do things without holding on to something.

Thankfully, I was coping a bit better with the world, and the incident didn't pull me back down into misery. If he was going to fall, then that would be his decision, be it conscious or unconscious. I realised that I couldn't prevent such things.

27

It was early February 2019, and the actual build had not yet begun on our apartment block. They were digging the basements, but it looked like the unit wouldn't be ready for us until mid- to late 2020. In a way, I was relieved that it would be a bit later than originally thought, because it would be extremely difficult to move house with Geoffrey's declining health.

I was still very much looking forward to it, however. As it was time for the developers to total up and order floor and wall tiles, benches, and other finishes, I went in to order the finishes for our apartment. It was exciting to think that it was becoming a reality. It was also a bit sad that I did this by myself, because Geoffrey would have no idea at all and wouldn't be able to make a considered choice about anything.

In the meantime, in our house, Geoffrey's bad eyesight and his uncoordinated movements meant that almost all the walls of the house had marks on them and scrapes where his walker had bruised the walls and the architraves. I seemed to be forever wiping finger-marks off the walls and the light switches. I was mentally totalling things up, because it was going to cost a bit to get fixed before I sold the house.

There was no point in doing any of this while Geoffrey was still bashing into the doorways and architraves and scraping his walker against walls. I didn't enjoy seeing the walls get knocked about, but I just had to be patient.

One day, when Geoffrey said something about the apartment and I told him that it was still a long way away, probably the middle or end of the following year, he promptly stated in a very matter-of-fact tone that he didn't think that he'd still be here by then.

———— ◆◦◆ ————

One Wednesday before Geoffrey came home from his bus trip, our dog groomer came with her van and was giving the dogs a bath and a tidy up. While I was handing over the dogs, our next-door neighbours were outside, and they came over to say hello. We stood under the tree right next to the dog groomer's van (it was a very hot day) and discussed various topics, including how Geoffrey was doing, when we might sell the house in order to move to the apartment, and when they were going on holidays in their caravan, which was currently on their front lawn.

Geoffrey arrived home, and the care worker wheeled him over to where we were. He was slightly in the sun, so after our neighbours gave him a quick greeting, we all made our way back inside our respective cool houses.

Once we were inside, Geoffrey asked who I had been talking to. I said that it was Peter and Di.

"Who?" he asked.

I repeated their names, and when Geoffrey looked confused, I added that they were our next-door neighbours.

"Oh, have they got a new van?" he asked.

I was initially a bit confused as to what he meant. I told him no; their normal caravan was still parked on the grass in front of their house as it had been for about a week or so because they were headed off for a holiday soon.

When Geoffrey then asked about the other van, I realised what he meant, and I told him that the van parked on the road belonged to Maria.

"Who?" he asked.

"Maria, the dog groomer. It's her van," I replied.

"What's she doing here?" was the next question.

"She's giving the dogs a bath today," I told him.

"OK," he said, "but who were the people you were talking to?"

"They are our next-door neighbours, Peter and Di," I repeated.

"Have they got a dog now?" was the next question.

I answered evenly, "No, it's *our* dogs the groomer is bathing."

He still looked a little confused, like he was going to continue with more of the same questions, but I quickly suggested that he relax. I asked him if he wanted ordinary tea or green tea. I made him a cup of tea, and the topic was forgotten.

Some days, Geoffrey was more with-it than others. On the not-so-good days, the above types of conversations were common.

Our garage door was finally replaced around the middle of February. It was lovely. It was quieter than the old one, and once the new one was installed, we could see just how much the old one had been faded. The new door made the front of the house look so much nicer, especially with the fact that the exterior of the house had been painted. What a bonus! I silently thanked the agency care worker who had damaged the old door. It had taken some time to get it replaced, but the trouble was worth it.

Finally, my appointment with the psychologist came around. I was certainly not feeling as bad as I had been over Christmas and early January when I'd made the appointment. I felt like a bit of a fraud because I was coping, mostly. Ah! It was the *mostly* which told me that I still needed some support. I was not 100 per cent all right. Usually when I had been talking to people, I had been saying that I was all right and coping well, but underneath, I knew this wasn't totally true.

It had been almost three years since Geoffrey had been diagnosed, and he had certainly deteriorated in that time. But as long as I was patient, things went along OK. The fact that I still had a huge sadness and frustration underneath everything meant that I was often not as patient as I could have been.

The tears erupted out of me almost as soon as I began to speak once I was in the psychologist's office. It had been over a year since I had seen her, and I clearly had some harsh judgements upon myself. She helped me to see how much nicer I could be to myself and how to calm my child-self and my teen-self when I found myself reacting badly to Geoffrey's actions or words. She also reminded me that it was OK to be sad. I was grieving for the person I had lost but who was still here.

I know the idea of seeing someone was to improve the situation, but I found that for forty-eight hours after the appointment, I almost felt worse before I was able to put some of the strategies into place and feel a bit better.

———◆———

I still found it hard to deal with Geoffrey in his 3-year-old-child brain space. He'd do something totally illogical, and when I'd stop him and point out the danger or the reason he didn't need to do it that way, he'd say innocently, "Oh, I didn't know" or "I didn't think of that." The old Geoffrey would have known or would have realised. I found myself sighing a lot.

One morning, when Geoffrey had attempted to drip some of my tea-tree oil into a tiny bottle he'd had breathe-easy oil in, I stopped him, pointing out that he was doing this over the carpet and the sink would be a better place. Also, he didn't want tea-tree oil, he wanted breathe-easy oil. When I received the usual 3-year-old response, I sighed and reminded him that he'd done this exact same thing before. I had been very cross that time, but he didn't remember, of course.

I told him that I was struggling with his 3-year-old brain today. I mimicked his response in a 3-year-old type of voice, and I made fun of him. He saw the funny side and had a big grin and a chuckle, and when I smiled at him and asked if he could see why I got frustrated, he nodded and grinned some more.

I said, "I know that you can't help it. It's just that part of your brain has reverted to being a 3-year-old, with no logic or sense."

"I know," he said. He paused and added, "I do love you."

"I love you too," I responded with a sigh.

***

I was looking forward to my next Melbourne trip, which was coming up in March of 2019. I had once again arranged for Geoffrey to go into respite for two weeks. When I returned from my trip, I would have three full days to myself before I collected him from respite. I had no special things that I wanted to do in that time, but I was looking forward to just having the house to myself and being able to please myself about everything.

Tamara was organising my schedule for Melbourne for me—a combination of seeing clients and spending time with family and friends. I would once again stay at Tamara's place with her beautiful dog. Just the thought of it helped me to feel good in the meantime, even though the couple of weeks prior was filled with commitments:

- We needed to see the doctor so that she could fill in the necessary forms for the care home.

- I had to get Geoffrey's medications and supplements packed by the chemist that the care home used.
- I had to ensure all his clothes and personal items were named.
- I had to pack for him and pack for myself separately.
- I had to ensure that I had enough money in our account to pay for the respite.
- I had to put a hold on his home care package carers from Blue Care.
- I had to also advise Liberty and cancel a couple of his bus trips.
- I had to arrange to give the keys and any relevant instructions to the dog-sitter/house-sitter.

Everyone has stuff which needs to be done prior to going away. Sometimes I felt that it was arduous because I was doing it all by myself and many of the jobs which needed doing were because of Geoffrey's condition.

Attempting to stay balanced and happy in the weeks leading up to my Melbourne trip was challenging. I chose to make use of some of my free time to tidy up and clean out some of the superfluous things in the house. I found that I had just stuffed things into the laundry cupboards, for example, so little by little I turned my attention to removing anything from those cupboards that I never used.

Usually I didn't have any problem at all in letting things go. I never liked hoarding things, and anything I deemed to be past its use-by date was easy to get rid of. Strangely, though, even as I knew I did not need all those bits and pieces, it was emotionally stressful trying to decide what to keep and what to get rid of. I thought that it was probably to do with my general state of mind, plus the fact there was still a certain amount of grief at my core.

I missed *my* Geoffrey. I had lost a great deal of him over the previous couple of years, and although in worldly terms I still had him with me physically, there was certainly a level of grief around having lost most of who he had been already.

———•◆•———

"I feel funny," Geoffrey said out loud.

It was around two in the morning, and I had been asleep. I was awakened by his words, but I wasn't sure what he'd said. I groggily asked him what he'd said, and he repeated it.

I made myself rouse to full consciousness and asked him in what way he felt funny. He needed to tell me exactly what was going on that made him feel that way. He just repeated that he felt funny.

Again, but this time with a small amount of alarm, I asked for clearer information. I needed to know what exactly he was feeling in his body, but he didn't say anything. I felt a bit concerned, but I waited.

After about a minute, he made an indistinguishable noise, and I asked him what was going on. He calmly answered that he had just farted, and now he felt better.

Oh great, I thought. *You woke me for a fart!* I sighed and, thankfully, swiftly went back to sleep.

———•◆•———

Geoffrey's middle daughter was having her sixtieth birthday in the middle of the year, and her husband phoned me to see if there was a chance that we could both come down to Melbourne for the day. He had planned for people to just "happen to come over to see her" on her birthday without planning a big surprise-type party.

I found myself having to explain to him the situation with Geoffrey. He hadn't realised that Geoffrey would not cope well with the airport and the travel, nor would he cope well with the change in routine, nor would he cope well with the lack of sleep, as he usually napped a lot throughout the daytime. Plus, we had nowhere to stay unless we stayed in a motel or apartment, because there was not enough room for Geoffrey to use his walker at Tam's place.

I would need the wheelchair as well, and I wasn't sure if the airline would take both his walker *and* a wheelchair. I was also unsure as to how I could get Geoffrey into their house, as the path was uneven, and there were a couple of steps at the door.

Although Geoffrey's son-in-law offered to help a little financially with the trip, it all added up to *too hard*. Sadly, I had to decline, as although I knew it would be a really great thing to be able do, I also knew that it would likely be disastrous. I would just be giving myself massive stress and struggle. This was much bigger than just a social outing. It was the right thing to say no, but I didn't feel good about it. I was a bit sad.

Any proposed social outing could cause huge problems, so mostly we didn't go anywhere together anymore. This created part of my trapped feeling. We were living on the Gold Coast. There were so many concerts and free public events on. Also, every week there were craft markets and art shows, plays, and more. Apart from the physicality of getting Geoffrey around not knowing how the parking or the disabled access would be, Geoffrey was just not up for crowds or noise, and he could no longer follow the plot of a play or a movie.

In some ways, I was lonely. I had lost Geoffrey's company, his fun, our chats, laughter, and outings together. I did make more of an effort to connect with people and to make better friendships. Oftentimes, I felt that I just didn't hit the mark. People seemed very caught up in their own lives, and I didn't feel as though I really fitted in.

I would arrange to have coffee with someone, and the person would forget and wouldn't turn up—or cancel because of some other event. I was determined to keep making an effort, as I knew that when Geoffrey died, I was going to need some friends. I kept hitting brick walls, though, and no matter what I tried, I felt as though I wasn't wanted or needed.

Admittedly, I had limited times when I could arrange things with anyone. It had to be a morning when I had a care worker at home with Geoffrey and I wasn't at the cafe working or at art class or at any personal appointments. This felt as though it was mirroring my childhood experiences, where I felt on the outside and that I had nothing to offer people. On the inside, part of me knew this wasn't true, and I knew that I was valuable and a worthy friend. It just wasn't working at that time.

I was alone and lonely. This caught me and contributed to my sad feelings too. I had to work really hard to feel good. I focused on my upcoming trip to Melbourne and knew that my friends there would welcome me and would go out of their way to spend time with me. I just needed a piece of that here at home as well.

28

For the Melbourne trip, I managed to book a rental car at around a third of the price from any car-rental companies with offices at the airport. Knowing I'd saved a considerable amount of money on the hire car, I made a bid on upgrading to business class for the trip to Melbourne. I got it and was overjoyed.

I took Geoffrey to the residential care home on the morning of my Melbourne trip, and he seemed OK and settled quite quickly. Paul took me to the airport, and I had plenty of time to relax in the Virgin Airlines lounge. It was so nice to have comfortable chairs and quality food and drink before my flight. I felt free, and I looked forward to the next two weeks before I had to collect Geoffrey and take him home.

The flight was lovely, and the meal on the plane was superb. I sighed with satisfaction. It was *so* nice to once again know that not only was flying business class a treat, Geoffrey was being well taken care of, and I had two whole weeks off.

The time I spent in Melbourne was delicious to say the least. I really enjoyed every minute I spent with Tamara and her beautiful dog, Harvey, and we genuinely had some quality time together. I caught up with a number of friends and relished every single conversation. I didn't get to see all my beautiful friends, but I thoroughly enjoyed eating out, special time spent with Nanna Jan, Darryl's fiftieth birthday party in the park, dinner cooked lovingly by Heather and Jayma, and spending some time with their adorable 2-year-old. There was so much laughter and fun with all of my soul family. Their hospitality and their support had no boundaries. I felt loved, cherished, and appreciated, and I soaked it all up.

Once again, I won a bid to upgrade my flight to business class on the flight home. There was lots of room on the plane and good service. I felt great. It was Sunday evening and pouring heavy rain on the Gold Coast when I arrived, but it didn't dampen my spirits one bit.

———◆———

While I was away, I had phoned Geoffrey every second day. On the Monday late afternoon when I phoned Geoffrey from home, I lied and told him that I'd only just arrived home that day and that I'd be going to bed early, doing washing, and catching up on stuff around the house on Tuesday. Wednesday would be work with clients at the cafe in the morning and a couple of clients at home in the afternoon. This was to ensure that he realised I was busy and I would pick him up on Thursday morning. I knew that I wasn't actually all that busy, but I had paid for two whole weeks, and I intended to make use of the full time I had by enjoying those few days at home on my own.

I had an appointment with my psychologist, and I talked with her about the guilt which haunted me—of feeling good about getting away, of not feeling good when I lied to him, and of feeling annoyed when he was acting like a child. She reminded me that Geoffrey's mind was deteriorating and yes, sometimes I had to treat him like a child. I wasn't looking forward to getting him home, and it was good to talk this through too.

There were so many things that Geoffrey could no longer do. He now found it impossible to do his crossword puzzles because not only was he having trouble seeing, he couldn't bring the words to mind. She had good suggestions about this, and I thought I'd do my best to follow her ideas through. They might give him something else that he could do. I came away feeling much better about the whole situation and felt as though I could manage once again.

I was able to fully enjoy and appreciate the few days I had to myself. On the Tuesday, I sat in a cafe, enjoyed a simply but yummy lunch, and wrote some more of this book. I took pleasure in being able to do this without having to rush because of a time that I had to be home by.

The morning that I was to collect Geoffrey from respite, I found myself dawdling. I just wasn't in a hurry to have him back. I think I was a bit anxious because I had categorically enjoyed my time off.

I arrived at the care home just after 9.30 a.m., and Geoffrey's face lit up when he saw me. I have to add here that this was an instant guilt stab for me. He was so happy to see me. He told me he loved me over and over and how much he missed me. All of that came out clearly, with no hesitation in his speech. As soon as I asked him anything, his speech was extremely halting, mumbling, and difficult to understand. I was a little surprised at my own mild irritation.

The first day home went along with nothing much of note. It was just doing the standard things which needed to be done for him. I took him out for a kebab lunch, and while he finished off his meal, since I had already eaten mine, I left him at the table and ducked into the supermarket to buy some supplies. I loaded up his wheelchair with the bags, and we made our way to the car. Apart from having to push a heavy load, it all went well.

Thankfully, the very next morning, I had a full three hours off, as a care worker came to shower Geoffrey, do a few things around the house, and take him out for coffee. He had awakened me several times during the night, and by the morning, I was tired again. It felt as though my two weeks off had really done me good, but the actual reality of life looking after Geoffrey had somehow slipped from my memory, and I wasn't fully expecting or remembering how much work he was.

He also seemed a little deafer. I found that I had to repeat everything three times before he heard what I was saying. I wasn't sure if that was my imagination or not. Perhaps, I thought, I used to automatically speak louder to him, and it was another thing which had been forgotten or wiped from my awareness. It all felt a bit weird.

Geoffrey was full of complaints about the care home this time. The food was great, but he complained about the nurses, he complained about the aides, he complained about not getting proper showers every day, and he complained about the activities being boring. The one activity he had wanted to go to was when there were animals/pets being brought in for a patting session for the residents. When the day and time came around for that session, he forgot about it, and so he had missed it.

In the end, I just said that I was sorry to hear that he hadn't enjoyed the time in respite but that I had really needed two weeks off, and that's just how it was. It didn't stop him from telling me about his complaints over and over again. I would just reply that it was a shame, and then I would change the subject.

———◆•◆•◆———

One of our nearby neighbours came over and invited me to a concert being held in a couple of days. She had been told by a friend who is in the chorus I had been in that I had a good bass voice, and they were looking for someone like me to join them. The concert was at two o'clock the following Saturday afternoon, and I found that I did very much want to go to it.

Saturday came, and Geoffrey was not up to going out. He was tired, and I had no one to come and stay with him (Lyn and Paul were still in Melbourne). I had wondered if Paul would perhaps be able to come over one evening a week to be with Geoffrey so I might be able to join if the chorus and their repertoire appealed to me. I did have a short moment of feeling hemmed in and trapped. I was disappointed to miss the concert. In order to feel OK, I had to focus on the fact that I'd have plenty of time for such things in the future. Right then and there, it was just too difficult.

The predictable pattern of daily life returned, and I was slowly able to manage it once again. I most definitely noticed how draining it was, and I made sure to enjoy my time off when the care workers were looking after Geoffrey. In this way, I was able to stay more balanced and happier within myself than I had before.

I wasn't sure what was different this time after my two weeks of respite, but somehow, I felt more balanced for longer after this recent Melbourne trip. I kept reminding myself that I was always looked after and that everything would work out in the end. ("If things are not worked out, then it is not yet the end!"—taken from a movie I once saw.)

Although Geoffrey had put on a little weight, most likely from the excellent meals and snacks at respite, he had less energy, slept more, chatted even less than usual, and needed the oxygen more often. He had clearly declined somewhat. Also, on some days, his speech was rather difficult to understand, and I had to be very patient in order to comprehend. Not only would his words fade off in volume, but often the words he was using or trying to use bore no resemblance to the message he was actually trying to express.

On numerous occasions, I would find our interactions hilarious, and I had to work hard not to laugh, because if I did that too often, he would get cross with me, and he'd give up attempting to get his words out in a sad, resigned type of way. I found this tough to deal with. Often when this occurred, I had to give myself some personal space to regain a place of balance.

Every now and again, Geoffrey would come out with some weird story that he would tell to me very sincerely. As soon as I realised it was not just that he was just mixing up his words and, in that moment, he really believed his fanciful story, I'd just agree with him or make murmuring, understanding noises, and he was happy.

Sometimes he would ask me if something had been done. The something could be anything at all, often something that didn't make any sense to me at all. I'd just repeat his question to make sure I was understanding and that once again he wasn't substituting a word that he couldn't think of, and then I'd tell him that yes, I'd done that something. It made him happy. Once again, quite funny but sad.

I also found myself to be somewhat amused but also quite sad when Geoffrey went into innocent mode. He would ask questions that were childlike or not logical. For example, I had been laboriously cleaning the grout in the floor tiles. Because I could not kneel on the floor, I was doing only about one square metre at a time, so it was slow going. Geoffrey looked at the floor tiles in the hallway which I hadn't done yet and suggested that we just get someone to come in with a pressure cleaner. When I pointed out that pressure cleaners were only for outdoor use, he said that he thought that if *he* had a mop close by, we could still use a pressure cleaner!

Another example of this was when we had watched a program on TV about the ambulance service taking people to hospital for various ailments. He asked if the ambulance would go back and get them to take them home again when the people were released from the emergency department. He was amazed when I said that no, usually, unless they were in aged care, people had to make their own way home or get someone to collect them, just like we had done in the past. He looked totally bamboozled. He had no memory of being taken to hospital and me having to get us home the next day—hence the reason I'd followed the ambulance to the hospital in my car.

———◆·◆·◆———

When I attended the next dementia carers' support group at Oz Care, they suggested that we use hand-cleaning gel for Geoffrey, as he was not washing his hands after using the toilet despite the fact that I knew his hands were often soiled. They even gave everyone a small bottle of it to try.

I'd been struggling to find activities which Geoffrey could manage. As I mentioned earlier, his eyes were deteriorating, and he'd totally given up on his crosswords and reading anything. At the support group meeting, I was also told about audiobooks, which we could obtain from the local library. I hadn't even thought about using the library. I hadn't used a local library since my children were young, so it hadn't even been on my radar. I immediately planned to go to the library with Geoffrey the very next day.

The library experience was interesting. I was told that I could log in with my library card details and download whatever audiobooks we wanted. The reality proved different. I was fairly tech-savvy, but it confused the heck out of me, and although once I was home again I did manage to download one audiobook, it seemed impossible to download the actual book that Geoffrey wanted, even though the screen information told me that the title was available as an audiobook. Oh dear; it was just another frustration to add to my list.

What increased the level of annoyance was that as I was trying to work out the system, Geoffrey kept asking me if I'd done it yet and could he help me? I was not feeling great, and I snapped at him. Then I felt worse.

Eventually, I realised that the book he wanted was available as an audiobook but not an e-audiobook. I downloaded something else for him, which he seemed happy about. He still needed me to stop it or restart it, but he was happy for a short while.

I did eventually become thoroughly sick of the situation with the e-books, because Geoffrey would inadvertently press a button and Siri would ask what he wanted. "How do I stop this stupid thing?" he would angrily call out. It didn't matter how often I warned him to keep his fingers away from the button, he still kept summoning Siri and complaining about the "stupid thing". His interest in listening to the stories waned within a couple of weeks. Thank goodness!

29

By early May 2019, Geoffrey had deteriorated considerably. He had seemed to go downhill over the previous six weeks or so. He was very breathless and found it hard to talk. Between that and the fact that the dementia made it hard for him to think of the words he needed, it was often very hard to understand him. I had to be *very* patient.

Very often, Geoffrey would say something incoherent, and when I'd ask what he'd said, he would look blankly at me and say that he couldn't remember. He would also ask me from time to time if he could help me with whatever task I was doing at the time, and he honestly thought that he would be able to just get up and help me to sweep, vacuum, clean, fold washing, or move furniture. I did at one time give him a pile of handkerchiefs to fold, which he struggled with but managed to do. The next time he asked me, I took some more from the drawer, shook them out, and gave them to him to fold. I could see that it made him feel useful. There was seemingly a never-ending pile of handkerchiefs to fold for whenever he wanted to help.

He was unable to shave himself, and at first, I was certainly not very good at doing it for him, but it became easier the more I did it. The toilet floor was soiled more and more often. I was already very competent at cleaning that up. He needed oxygen most of the time, and we began to use the oxygen cylinder when he was away from home. The oxygen converter was running about eighteen hours a day. He was not eating a great deal and had lost weight again.

The cardiologist said, at the regular visit, that I should look into palliative care. Even though we didn't need that yet, he suggested that we get the referral done and get started to set up the process, as it could take some time. In this way, I would only need to make a phone call when the time came. We would have a choice of care at home or in the palliative care ward in Robina Hospital.

I knew that it had to be at home. I'd rather Geoffrey was in familiar surroundings when he passed, and I knew he wasn't at all keen on being in the hospital for anything. I didn't have a problem with someone dying in my house, because I saw it as a privilege. It would be a privilege to have a birth in your home, and I saw a death as the same.

Many years ago, my lovely friend Kath and her husband, Peter, were living with us when Peter became very ill and, in turn, needed palliative care. He ultimately passed away in the comfort of our home in Melbourne. I really appreciated the understanding and care which came from our beautiful friendship. Thank you, Kath. I love you.

Toileting was a problem. The dementia meant that Geoffrey could not think logically, so when his urine flow started before he was on the toilet, he wouldn't just hitch his pull-ups back up and urinate in them but rather pull his pull-ups down and just keep urinating on his clothes or the floor until he was able to sit down on the toilet. When he made a urine mess on the bedroom carpet as well as every item of clothing he was wearing, I was not impressed! He needed a full change of clothes twice a day. It was hard work.

No matter how many times I reminded him, he was just not able to plan or think clearly around this issue. I bought a second urine bottle so that he could have one next to his chair and he could use that rather than trying to get all the way to the toilet. I knew that I was risking him soiling the chair, but his ability to mobilise had deteriorated, and it was taking him longer to get to the toilet. I knew that I'd be getting those chairs recovered when I moved anyway. It was a calculated risk.

———◆•◆•◆———

Catherine, my beautiful friend, came from Melbourne to stay for a few days. She was a wonderful support, as Geoffrey was deteriorating by the day. It was hard to understand much when he spoke. He needed the oxygen on for twenty-four hours a day; he was coughing up phlegm and struggling to breathe.

The visit to the GP for the palliative care referral did not go as I expected. Once the doctor saw him, she would not let me take him home. She phoned for an ambulance to take him to hospital. She completed the paperwork we needed for the palliative care team but insisted she could not let him go home as he was.

Catherine headed back to Melbourne on the Wednesday after doing some housework and cooking up a big pot of soup for us. Thank you, Catherine. I love you.

Four days in hospital with intravenous diuretics saw Geoffrey back to where he had been a couple of months earlier health-wise: coughing but only a little, on oxygen only a few hours a day, and breathing a bit easier. Cognitively, though, there was no doubt that he had declined.

The only change to his medication was a prescription for some liquid morphine, one millilitre to be given every six hours as required to help him sleep and to relieve discomfort from being unable to breathe easily. The hospital doctors made it clear that this had been a one-off and that to give such high doses of diuretics over again would seriously compromise his kidneys, and that would make everything worse. Next time he declined to this state, he would be transitioned to palliative care.

Before Geoffrey came home from hospital, I took the opportunity to sell our king-sized bed, because he had been finding it very hard to get into (it was very high), and it was becoming dangerous. I had intended to sell it at some stage before I moved into the apartment anyway. With Paul's help—thank you, Paul—I moved the queen bed into our room from the second bedroom and then moved the double bed from the fourth bedroom into the second bedroom. What a bed shuffle!

The trouble was, Geoffrey was used to the space that the king bed had given us. When he rolled over in the queen bed, he took up three quarters of it. I slept perched on the very edge of the bed each night; otherwise, he would smash into me every time he turned.

Fiona and the children came to stay for the Mother's Day weekend, and we had a lovely time. As Catherine had done the previous week, Fiona pushed Geoffrey in the wheelchair around the market on Sunday morning, only this time, he did not need to have the oxygen tank with him. On the Saturday night, he had awakened me at 2 a.m., asking if I was going to get up because we had to go to the market. I told him that it was two in the morning and way too early to get up, and he went back to sleep.

Geoffrey slept a lot throughout each day, and he did not cope very well when the children became a little loud, which children are wont to do. In reality, they were not very loud children, so it wasn't a problem. They were actually very responsive to the fact that Pa couldn't cope with loud noises. When they left to go home on the Sunday evening, they both gave Geoffrey really big hugs, and both of them looked him in the eye and said, "I love you, Pa." He told them that he loved them too. It was very touching.

Six days after his return from hospital, I gave Geoffrey his first dose of the morphine liquid. He did sleep better and didn't need the oxygen for most of the night. I gave him his dose every evening, but that was all at that stage.

How was I? Well, I found that I was very up and down emotionally. I stayed balanced and coped with almost everything. Then, some extra little thing would occur, often something which was easily remedied, and I would break down in tears and be quite unreasonable in my thinking. I knew that I was not thinking clearly, but I did not have the strength or capacity to do much about it.

The Monday after Mother's Day weekend, I totally forgot that it was Monday, and I failed to turn up to my Pilates class. When my beautiful Pilates teacher contacted me to see if I was all right, I realised that it was Monday and what I'd done. I was shocked that I could have forgotten. The carer had come just as usual, and I had toddled off to do errands and so forth without any thought at all about my Monday Pilates class.

Two days later, on Wednesday, after I had seen some clients at the cafe, I had an appointment to get my nails done. This was something I did every month, but this time I struggled to get there because I found myself driving along, and suddenly I had no idea where I was going. I mean, I really had *no clue* about how to get there. I pulled the car over, and I felt lost. Momentarily I didn't know where I was or where I was going. It was scary.

After a couple of deep breaths, I managed to remember where I was going, but it took a little longer for me to figure out exactly *where* I had to go. I arrived eventually, and although I had been going to this place for years, I found it hard to find the exact house in the street. I realised that I was seriously stressed.

My poor brain was overloaded and was doing an emergency shutdown on me. That evening, I phoned, my wonderful art teacher. I told her what was going on and arranged to take a break from the art classes. Although I loved doing my art, I did not have any passion or inspiration for it at that time. Thank goodness she understood. Then I did the same with my Pilates teacher.

I intended to keep the carers coming to look after Geoffrey for those times, and I'd use those hours to relax, listen to music, have coffee, write this book, and in general, just have time off. Obviously, I was stressed, but at the same time, I felt all right in many ways. It was very weird.

INSIGHT - SIXTEEN

Stress can be described as a type of psychological pain. Positive stress can help us become motivated, and it can help us to react as required to our environment, so it's not all bad. But it is also reported that continued high levels of stress can increase the risk of diseases such as strokes, heart attacks, ulcers, and more.

Stress is triggered by internal perceptions of *not enough* (such as *I'm not enough, there's not enough money/time/resources/help*, etc.). This causes us to experience anxiety or other negative emotions regarding situations, such as pressure, discomfort, and so on. We all experience stress or perceive things as threatening from time to time—some more than others. In essence, when we feel or perceive that whatever is being demanded of us is greater than our ability to cope, we then feel stress.

There have been many books written on the subject of how to relieve stress, but essentially, we need to understand and be aware of what we are doing in order to do something differently. When we feel stressed, it is often because we are trying to do too much or we feel pressured. This is a result of an internal drive that we should do or be more. In reality, we are not physically or mentally able to achieve the *more* we are pressuring ourselves to do.

When we realise that we are in command of our feelings, we begin to see that we have choices and can relieve our stressful feelings. The first step to doing this is creating a space for ourselves. Start by taking slow, deep breaths. Imagine yourself in your happy place, such as the beach, forest, or mountains. Acknowledge the good things in life and be grateful.

Questioning ourselves is a powerful tool and is the next step in relieving our stressful feelings. Asking ourselves about where we have high expectations of ourselves, especially as carers, is a good start. Are we expecting to be able to keep our loved one safe every minute of the day? This is common for carers and adds a great deal of pressure.

Actually, what we need to do is back off a little and allow our loved ones some space to do what they can or what they want, as much as possible—even when we see that what they are doing could be dangerous and that they could fall, for example. There is only so much we can do. If we do not take an excess amount of responsibility for them, we can allow them to make their own mistakes.

This was very difficult for me, as I was sure that Geoffrey was going to fall and break a bone or something. The result was that he felt controlled, and I felt stressed with the need to be hyper-aware of everything he was doing every minute of the day. What I needed to do was to let go of the fear that it would be my fault if he got hurt. This is a big fear amongst carers, and we need to let go just a little.

It's just as you would do with a child. You have to allow people to make their own mistakes and live with the consequences. This can be very hard to do when you love someone and only want to protect that person. Regularly reminding ourselves that we are doing the best that we can do and that is OK takes away a measure of the pressure we put upon ourselves. The secret, I found, is to do this often.

30

On 17 May 2019, the community palliative care nurse came for an assessment visit. She was wonderful, understanding, and empathetic, and she saw the need to get Geoffrey off the cycle of being good at home and then deteriorating, having to go to hospital, having intravenous diuretics, getting better, going home, and within seven to ten days, heading back to hospital for the same thing again. I did not want to get into that cycle. That was not good for anyone, and each time Geoffrey deteriorated, he became more and more scared. It was awful to watch.

She gave me a letter to give to the ambulance service if we needed to call an ambulance again, instructing them that he was under the palliative care team.

Geoffrey had commented a couple of times that he wished he had belief in how I had explained what I thought heaven was. He was clearly feeling a bit worried.

My son, Mick, came up from Melbourne that afternoon for a few days, and we had a great time. Mick did some serious work in the garden and improved it enormously. On the Sunday, he pushed Geoffrey in his wheelchair around the market. Although the outing really tired Geoffrey out, he enjoyed Mick's company a great deal, and Mick was able to make Geoffrey laugh out loud many times. It was an absolute delight.

That evening, Mick took my car and went and collected Tamara from the airport. Geoffrey didn't want to go to bed until Tamara arrived, but her plane would not land until at least 9.30 p.m., and Geoffrey was very ready for bed long before that. I managed to convince him that Tamara would understand and that he would see her in the morning. Settling him was difficult, and he called me back into the bedroom a couple of times for very minor things.

On the third call, I asked him what it was he really needed, and he quietly said that he wanted me to sit with him until he fell asleep.

"Sure," I said, and I lay down beside him on top of the blankets and held him until he was asleep. It did pull at my heartstrings. He was so scared and vulnerable.

It was so beautiful to have Mick and Tamara there together. I felt very supported, and they had some beautiful interactions with Geoffrey. Some of them were hilarious, as Geoffrey became more confused and kept losing the plot. There was no sign of any awkwardness about this, as Mick had the knack of knowing exactly what to say to make Geoffrey laugh. It was great. Thank you, Mick. I love you.

———◦●◦———

That evening, when Tamara had not even been there twenty-four hours, Geoffrey took a turn for the worse. Mick and Tam had moved one of the single beds into our bedroom so that I might be able to get a good night's sleep. Geoffrey was not happy that I was not in the same bed, but I was being disturbed a great deal in the queen bed with him. In the single bed, I was still in the same room, thanks to the fact that our bedroom was a generous size, but he took some convincing.

He had been coughing considerably, and by the time we both settled into bed, his breathing was laboured and raspy. He said he was OK, and I turned over. Just as I was drifting off, I became aware that he had turned on his bedside lamp. I heard a slight whoofing noise, and I glanced over my shoulder to discover that he was on the floor.

He had sat on the edge of the bed with a view to using his urine bottle but had slipped to the floor.

He was wedged awkwardly in the corner between the bed and the bedside table. I could not get him up. I called out for Mick, and he and Tamara managed to get him over onto his hands and knees and support him in getting up. He hadn't hurt himself at all, and after he used the bottle, I resettled him in bed.

I returned to my bed, but within a few minutes, Geoffrey was seriously distressed. He called out to me that he couldn't breathe. He was very agitated and panicked. We couldn't calm him down, and we ended up calling an ambulance. He told me shakily that he was scared of dying. It was apparent he had forgotten all the spiritual information we'd worked with over the years.

He was admitted to Robina Hospital again. They pumped him full of diuretics, and over the course of about four days, he recovered enough that he could have gone home. What halted this was that I realised I couldn't manage him at home. My back was seriously complaining about all the physical assistance I'd been giving him, and I was exhausted. As I mentioned earlier, I couldn't see the point of this cycle of home and then deteriorating, to hospital then lots of diuretics, home and then deteriorating, to hospital again ad infinitum. The medical team finally heard my plea, and a meeting was promised to work out what to do moving forward.

Mick had flown home the afternoon after Geoffrey was admitted to hospital. He knew there was a good chance that he would not see Geoffrey alive again. He said his goodbye and acknowledged all the things Geoffrey had done for him. He told Geoffrey how much he loved him. It was emotionally painful but also very real and touching.

Tamara was, of course, wonderful and cooked her heart out in order to put some ready meals into the fridge and freezer for me. It was a godsend!

I had contacted Geoffrey's three daughters and told them how sick he was, and they all arranged to come visit. Erin arrived first from New Zealand, and Geoffrey was really delighted to see her. Then the others arrived from Melbourne, and he was surprised and touched by their presence.

Geoffrey was moved to the palliative care ward, and the following day, we finally had the family conference meeting that we'd been told we needed to have. It was with the palliative care team, the medical team, and the social worker. The four girls and myself all ended up in tears, of course, as the decision to stop active care for Geoffrey and to just make him comfortable was a tough one.

We all knew, however, that it was the most generous decision for him. None of us wanted to see him as distressed as he was the night that he was brought into hospital ever again. Within two days of that meeting, the girls all left to go home. Each of them had time with Geoffrey to say goodbye, and although it was hard, each was very real, honest, and open with her parting words. There were many tears, hugs, and loving conversations.

In a way, it was good that he had picked up considerably with all the medication and was with-it enough to participate, understand, and reply to their loving communications. It was emotionally draining, but I was very thankful that they all had that very special time with him.

———◆———

On the Thursday, I was able to take Geoffrey home for a couple of hours so that he could see the dogs. Benny, a dog that didn't like to be on your lap, stayed on Geoffrey's lap for about five minutes, which is quite something. Missy, a lap dog through and through, spent over an hour on Geoffrey's knee, and he loved it.

I made sure I was at the hospital early each day so that I could be there when the doctors saw him. Because he wasn't seen every day, it was five days after the meeting, and Geoffrey was still being given a considerable amount of diuretics (frusemide). On the Friday, I demanded that he see a doctor, because his frusemide dose needed to be lowered. I also suspected that he had a UTI.

That day, the catheter was removed, and a urine sample was taken. They also moved him to a medical ward that afternoon because he was too well to be in the palliative care ward. Of course, he was well right then—he was still on a fair amount of medication! I thought that at the family meeting, we had been heard about the fact that he would be good for about seven days or so after withdrawal of the meds and then he would go down fast. But the system didn't seem to work well, and every time he was seen by a doctor, it was a different one. They didn't seem to read the notes, and I had to go through everything all over again.

After he had been in the medical ward for three days, the doctor who saw him told us that he did indeed need antibiotics for a UTI. Then he confidently said, "He can probably go home tomorrow!"

I had to explain in front of Geoffrey once again that there was no way I could cope with him at home anymore. I couldn't manage. Although in the previous few days Geoffrey was very understanding as to why I couldn't manage him at home anymore, the doctor's words that morning set him off into a barrage of questions as to why he couldn't go home.

One thing he wanted to know was what I needed in order for him to come home. The reality was that even with someone else being there twenty-four hours a day, which seemed impossible, I wasn't convinced that I could do it anymore. I had done some serious damage to my back, and I knew that I needed to get some treatment for it. I ended up having a few physiotherapy treatments and some Bowen therapy. I actually continued with treatment for several months before my pain went down to anywhere near a manageable level.

I really did feel bad about Geoffrey having to go to an aged care residence. There was certainly a level of shame within me. It wasn't just that I felt a bit guilty over the whole situation, but my beautiful psychologist had uncovered shame. Inside me, there was shame that I couldn't fix it all, that I couldn't do it all. I expected myself to be able to do everything. Plus, my inner child-self had been programmed that I was a bad girl if I didn't have everything sorted all by myself. It was difficult to explain.

To you, the reader, I'd say that many people probably feel this way, and it's hidden and well buried inside. I knew, for me, that the feelings of shame stemmed from my stressful childhood experiences. Once I uncovered this, I was able to consciously put it down and choose to feel better. This wasn't an instant thing, however, and I needed to remind myself regularly that it was OK to have reached my limit and it was OK to say that I could no longer look after Geoffrey.

INSIGHT – SEVENTEEN

The guilt/shame feelings we hold usually stem from our childhood somewhere. If you have guilt or shame feelings, were you blamed or abused? Did you feel, or do you feel, responsible for fixing everything? Do you feel that you have to do everything, or most things, on your own? When we are running these beliefs or thoughts, we often take on an excess amount of responsibility, and this pushes us to do things well—or what we may see as properly.

This can be a motivator in our lives in a good way, but it can also push us beyond what is sensible, and we overachieve or overextend ourselves. Often, this feeling puts us in the position of never wanting to give up, because we can see giving up or ceasing whatever we are doing as failure.

It's our child-self that sees failure. In reality, it is not failure; it is simply being an adult and knowing when we have done as much as we can do and it is time to let go the reins. Being run by guilt and/or shame can also be what stops us from allowing support or assistance. You will recognise this by the language of *should*, *have to*, and *must* in your thoughts and words. When we put ourselves into situations where we feel as though we should or we must or we have to do certain things, we find, if we look deeply within ourselves, that there is childhood fear and feelings of guilt or shame if we can't do it all by ourselves.

Understanding our inner motivators behind should, have to, and must begins to give us freedom from these old ties. We need to understand that these old drivers don't diminish who we are in any way. Rather, the awareness and acknowledgment of them frees us up to be loving to ourselves and others. It allows us to ask for and receive assistance when we need it.

Remember how good you feel when you are able to help someone in some way? So it goes that when you allow others to help you, you are not failing. What you are doing is allowing someone else the opportunity to feel good as a result of helping someone. This is not failure; it is generosity to others and to yourself.

That week, I fell. I tripped over a concrete block in the car park of some shops. I winded myself. I smashed my left knee hard, banged my head on the concrete pavement, and grazed my cheekbone. Fortunately, I was able to get someone's attention, and as she ran over to me, she alerted some workmen who also came to my aid.

They offered to call an ambulance, but I didn't feel that was necessary. They obtained some fresh water for me to drink and helped me up. They did not leave me until they were reassured that I was all right. Nothing was broken, but I felt miserable and hopeless. I just cried. The fall had seriously made my back a lot worse, and it was hard not to feel sorry for myself.

31

Geoffrey was moved back to the palliative care ward, but he was not considered one of their patients; he was still a medical patient. When I asked to see the social worker, I thought it would be the one I'd dealt with before, but it was a different person from the ones who had been in on the family meeting. I found that I had to explain everything again. Didn't anyone read the notes on file?

Because the staff could only see that Geoffrey was fairly well, or at least was stable, I was told that he couldn't just stay in hospital. The social worker suggested that I look at care homes to see if I could use up the respite allowance that Geoffrey still had (about six weeks) with a view to taking up a permanent place when one became available. Part of me felt as if that was all an exercise in uselessness, because based upon past experience, I was truly not convinced that Geoffrey would stay well or stable much past another week after he had been taken off his meds. Nevertheless, I organised six inspections of care homes over the next few days.

Geoffrey had told me one morning that he had been given formaldehyde instead of frusemide. That made me giggle! He also told me that one of the nurses had refused to shower him. All that had happened was that there was some sort of emergency, and she had dashed off and told him that she would be back to shower him, but a different nurse had returned to do the job. In his mind, the first nurse had refused to shower him. No amount of explaining would change his mind.

As usual, he was slow to respond to questions or requests, and he struggled a little with the TV control. Mostly, though, he appeared to be high-functioning, at least as far as the staff were concerned. Geoffrey had been in hospital about two weeks by then, and it was clear that he was indeed picking up. Each day I saw him, he was better than before.

———————

Looking at the residential care homes, I immediately ruled out the one Geoffrey had been in for respite, as he clearly was not happy there. I found the first one I went to see to be good, bright, and clean, with happy residents, good meals, and a great activities program—but they had no places available.

The second place I viewed was awful. Actually, awful is an understatement! The residents' rooms were tiny and featureless, with empty walls, no shelves at all, nothing. There was old lino in the hallway, lino in the rooms, cramped entrances, and no space to swing a mouse, never mind a cat! The living and dining rooms were dark and the furniture looked shabby. The activities program looked depressing, and I felt very disheartened to say the least. Although they had rooms available, I very strongly said no thank you to that one.

The next one that I saw was beautiful and close to home. It had good-sized rooms with lovely outlooks, nice gardens, pleasant indoor and outdoor spaces to sit, and light and comfortable lounge and dining areas. There was a great activities calendar and a good menu. When I met some of the residents, they were chatty and happy. I thought that was a good sign. Although this care home shot to the top of my list, alas, they too had no beds available.

The next place, I decided, was a bit far away. It was fair to middling in my comparisons, but the distance ruled it out anyway.

Then I found Cedarbrook, run by Carinty. It was close to home and only eighteen months old. It had lovely staff and happy residents. It was bright, light, and airy, with good rooms, lovely gardens, and a semi-rural outlook from every window. There were good activities and chef-prepared meals. And *yes!* They had a room available.

I felt so relieved. I cancelled the viewing for the final place I was supposed to go and see. I felt that I had found the best place. Against all odds, Geoffrey was still improving, and when I showed him the brochure for Cedarbrook, his first comment was, "It looks lovely. When do I go there?"

The next day, I had to get an appointment with our GP so she could fill in the appropriate paperwork. I filled in all the other necessary papers and returned them to Cedarbrook that day. I was quite exhausted, physically and emotionally.

Over that weekend, I spent less time with Geoffrey at the hospital and more time at home resting. I caught up on some sleep, too, which was essential. The time I did spend with him showed me that he was more with-it than he had been for a while, and he was meandering down the corridors with a four-wheel walker. He was bright, cheery, and giving cheek to the nurses, just like the old days.

For sure, his memory was not fabulous, but he appeared to be a lot better. I did wonder whether maybe he might have been overmedicated previously so that now he was off almost everything, he was better. Hmm, wasn't that an interesting thought? It was still a day-to-day process. Each day I visited, I thought I had no expectations, but I was surprised each time that he seemed so well.

The day after I had accepted a place at Cedarbrook for Geoffrey, a place became available at the first care home I'd looked at. Too late! I was very happy with my choice of Cedarbrook.

———◆———

It took a week from the time I accepted a place at Cedarbrook for Geoffrey until they were able to admit him. It was a very long week. He was champing at the bit to get out of hospital, and he just wanted to come home.

I felt awful. I was severely judging myself for not wishing to take him home. I knew I was burnt out, overwhelmed, and totally spent. At the same time, though, I still had that little voice inside telling me that I was a bad person because I was saying no. The internal struggle made me feel vulnerable, and tears were never very far from the surface. I wondered if I would feel all right ever again.

There was no doubt that I was extremely happy with my choice of care home for Geoffrey. It was bright, clean, and homely. The staff were friendly, helpful, caring, and cheerful. The corridors were carpeted and wide. The rooms were spacious and well-appointed, and the television was fairly large, so it was easy for Geoffrey to see. There were plenty of wardrobe space, drawers, and shelving. His room overlooked both the car park and bushland. He was pleased because he enjoyed watching people come and go.

There were several lounge rooms, a large balcony, and gardens to choose from when he wanted to be elsewhere. Each had a different view over fields and bushland. The motorway could also be seen from some, and this provided more movement to watch. People walked their dogs and children rode their minibikes along one of the fields, and Geoffrey enjoyed watching their antics.

He was not in the dementia section, as he was much more with-it ,
than not, especially now that he had picked up. His fellow residents
were a mixture of able-bodied and not; cognitively, there was also
a great range. This also meant there were people who were chatty,
and so he could listen or join in conversations around him, which he
appreciated. It took him a while to settle in and find his way around,
but as they had different corridors painted different colours, even in
the early days it was easy for him to go down the teal-coloured corridor
in order to find his room.

I had spent some time talking with him, before he was admitted,
about how important it was to participate in the exercise group every
morning and that it would help to keep his body strong and build up
his muscles again. Also, I stressed how important it was for his mind
and brain function to participate in the other activities. By the time
Geoffrey was there, he happily participated in almost everything which
was offered. I understood that he needed to see the point or needed to
see the possible benefit in doing things; otherwise, he wasn't interested.

Every Tuesday morning, a group of sweet kindergarten children
came in, but Geoffrey decided on the first Monday that he wasn't going
to bother going to that because he said that it didn't interest him. It
took a bit of talking for him to see that there were possible benefits,
and he might enjoy himself. Children expressed joy, and he could do
with some of that. It would give his brain stimulation just watching
the children playing.

The next day, when I visited, I discovered that he did go to the
session with the children, but he'd fallen asleep and it wasn't of interest
to him. *Oh well*, I thought, *you can't win them all!*

Once a month, there was a "men's shack" activity, and Geoffrey
looked forward to that. When he attended, he did enjoy it immensely.
The first time he attended, he was given a small stool to paint. His

coordination was terrible, and it was a real struggle for him to paint it evenly. But he enjoyed the banter, the camaraderie, and the sense of achievement. It was so heartening for me. It confirmed to me, yet again, that he was in the place that was best for him.

32

I had been receiving phone calls, text messages, Facebook messages, and more from friends and family. I mostly just chatted to very few people here and there, because I just didn't feel that I had the energy to have lots of conversations. It was lovely to know that so many people, both in Melbourne and the Gold Coast, were thinking of me and were sending love and caring.

I felt somewhat disconnected, though. I was happy with my own company most of the time; however, the first Saturday afternoon after Geoffrey went into care, I did go to a casual social get-together, and I enjoyed it a lot. The fact that there was no pressure, just relaxing chat and getting to know some new people, made it very comfortable. This group of people, all of whom had spiritual beliefs similar to my own, decided to get together monthly, and I looked forward to the next one.

Slowly, I began to get the house cleaned and sorted and to do the jobs I had put on hold when Geoffrey was in hospital. It was hard to get motivated, and I had to ensure that I only tackled one main task per day, or I would feel so overwhelmed that I'd procrastinate and then do nothing at all. I visited Geoffrey every day, spending a couple of hours with him, mostly in the afternoons so that he had a chance to do the morning activities.

I told Geoffrey that I needed a couple of weeks to get myself together, and then I would take him out on the weekends. I planned to take him out for lunch or for a drive to the hills or the beach or to take him home for a short visit. I knew that we needed some time for him to adjust and some time for me to feel better before I could do that.

I was taking care of my back, and it was slowly feeling a little better. In terms of Geoffrey's health, it was most perplexing that he was so much better with hardly any medication at all, and the only supplement he was taking was one vitamin C a day. He had almost no sign of heart failure, except for a slight cough and a little swelling of his ankles.

Dementia-wise, he appeared better in some ways. He still forgot things and still was not communicating well. He would forget words and people's names. I thought that some of his improvement was that he was living in a place where all his needs were taken care of. He had a printed activities schedule which he could refer to as often as he wished. The staff came to tell him, no matter where he was, that a meal was about to be served or an activity was about to start, and his belongings were all in one room and easy to find.

At home, he was often anxious about things: When was this or that happening? Had I remembered about this or that? Had I put the bins out? Had I bought cream? Could I find his glasses? When was the podiatrist coming? Which carer was coming? When was dinner going to be ready? Once again, when I thought about many of these anxieties being removed, I acknowledged that he was in the best possible place.

When I visited, he always said that he missed me. Sometimes I would stay for a meal with him, which he enjoyed, as he also liked that I chatted with the other residents. One of the ladies only spoke French, and when I realised this, I was able to have small conversations with her in my long-ago, almost forgotten, minimal French. Geoffrey looked at me in amazement and said, "I didn't know you could speak French." I grinned and told him that he should know by now that I was full of surprises! He laughed.

Often, we would spend time in one of the lounges which had a jigsaw puzzle on a table, available for anyone to use. After spending some time looking out the window at the view, the activity, or just the weather, Geoffrey would look through the jigsaw pieces to find me certain colours, and I'd put the puzzle together. He liked to feel useful, and we'd chat a bit. He loved that I still kissed him and would give him cuddles. He seemed to understand that I couldn't be there all day, but he would have liked me to do just that.

———————•◆•———————

Over the next few weeks, Geoffrey settled in more and more. He gradually began to call Cedarbrook home. I had explained, on several occasions, just how important it was to keep his body fit and able, and he should go to morning exercises. He would attend daily, and he enjoyed them. Once I explained how important it was to do whatever he could to keep his mind active, he would also attend some of the other things, such as word games and other interactive sessions.

When he said he was no good at the ball games so he wouldn't go to them anymore, I managed to get him to see that it was what he needed in order to strengthen his muscles and retune his coordination. Amazingly, he agreed and began to attend the ball games, Nerf target games, and more. What is important here is that he not only remembered my advice but discovered that he loved these activities. His favourite monthly activities, though, were the men's shack and the drumming sessions. It was a whole new life for him, and for me.

Geoffrey refused to tell me that he was happy there. Instead, he'd tell me how much he missed me or that his preference was to be at home with me. This really tugged at my heartstrings, and I'd feel incredibly sad. Sometimes I couldn't help but cry, and I had to remind myself that he, and I, were better off with him in care.

———◆———

In July 2019, my beautiful soul family came up from Melbourne, and over a couple of weeks, I had a very full house. On the Sunday that we had a big gathering, I collected Geoffrey from Cedarbrook and brought him home for the day. Everyone had contributed to lunch, and we had a magnificent feast. Geoffrey enjoyed it immensely. He went to bed after lunch and had a good sleep, and then he was able to participate some more. He loved that everyone looked after his every need. I returned him to Cedarbrook in time for him to have dinner there. He was very tired.

Personally, I fully enjoyed having everyone stay with me. We ate out a number of times. Even when we were all at home, others would prepare the meals, and I felt very cared for. Everyone contributed something: good company, emotional support, groceries, physical help to do things around the house, and money. After all the laughter and fun, it was extremely quiet when everyone left, but I felt good.

I continued to have treatments for my back, but it still gave me grief, and I continued to take the painkillers just so that I could function. The doctor sent me for X-rays and a CT scan, which showed that all the discs in my lumbar spine were bulging; there was also some age-related deterioration. The pain was continuous, but I wasn't prepared to go down the cortisone injections or the surgery route.

I arranged to have some Bowen therapy every week, and that seemed to work, although I knew it wasn't going to be fixed immediately and that the healing process would take some time. The doctor suggested that acupuncture might reduce the pain. I attended a clinic and had a total of six acupuncture sessions with no change at all in the pain level, so I returned to the weekly Bowen therapy treatments, which seemed to be working. Nevertheless, it was a slow process.

I had a painter come and paint all the walls, doors, and architraves. This had the effect of lightening and brightening the whole house. It looked clean and fresh.

I had sold some furniture already, and I pushed myself to get organised. I made a list of the rest of the things for sale which I would not be needing in the future. I organised a garage sale for early in September and slowly worked my way through the house, removing as many things as possible that I thought I could let go of. I had the pool filter fixed and had the concrete out the back cleaned and repainted.

The garage sale went very well, with the help of three of my beautiful soul family who came up from Melbourne to help me for several days, plus a strong young man I knew here on the Coast. Before the ladies went back to Melbourne, they helped to style the house for me for the photos which would be put online. It was *so* enormously supportive of them all, and I knew I'd be forever grateful.

I still visited Geoffrey six days a week (I wasn't visiting on Wednesdays), and I kept him informed of the progress of the house preparation and sale. Occasionally, when he was having a good day, he'd say that he wished that he could help me. On a bad day, he could barely concentrate on what I was saying, and he hardly spoke at all.

Some days he would want to tell me something—for example, at exercises. He would say three words, and then I'd just get, "ah … and ah … ah … ah" for several minutes as he struggled to get words from his brain to his mouth. Some days he was totally unable to tell me anything that I understood. From a physical perspective, though, he had gained weight and was looking good. Although a little wobbly when he initially stood up, he would walk with his walker at a good pace.

I was much more able to cope with Geoffrey's dementia since he went into care. I no longer took things personally, as I was not having to cope with him twenty-four hours a day. I was sleeping better (not being awakened in the night), and I had more time to rest, heal, and do whatever I chose for the majority of each day. Overall, I would say that we were both happier. Our needs were being met.

Geoffrey loved that I went in and spent time with him. Sometimes we chatted, and sometimes I just sat with him—in his room, in one of the lounges, or on the balcony. I'd make us a cuppa at times or I'd take him out, at least once a week. He appeared to be a much happier version of himself than when I was looking after him myself at home. I was so relieved.

I put the house on the market with a very experienced real estate agent, and she kept me informed all the way through the process. During my visits with Geoffrey, I kept him informed about what was going on with the house. I brought him home one day to show him how nice everything looked, and it gave him a chance to say goodbye to our home.

33

On 5 October 2019, it was Geoffrey's eighty-eighth birthday. A colourful banner wishing him happy birthday had been placed on the door of his room. He loved it. The staff had sung to him the previous day at the afternoon concert; I think he was quite chuffed about that too.

I made sure that he had a good birthday. I took a cake in to him, gathered up a couple of his new friends, and the four of us had a lovely morning tea on the front patio of the care home. We sang "Happy Birthday" and chatted and laughed. It was quite lovely to get to know his friends a little more. I took him to his favourite pub for lunch, and then we drove through the countryside for a while. He thoroughly enjoyed the day and was very tired when I returned him to Cedarbrook.

The next week, I took him to have his annual hearing aid adjustments. He was most pleased to be able to hear properly again.

It was a busy time for me. I'd organised for a pool safety certificate to be done. I'd sold some items on Facebook Marketplace. I'd sent some things to St Vincent de Paul Society and just generally cleaned out excess items. I decided that some things I no longer needed could be sold after I moved into the house I was going to share until my apartment was ready.

I kept my home clean and well presented for all house inspections, which was a bit tiresome, but thank goodness, it only took just over a month to sell. Tamara came up from Melbourne the second weekend, and she was a huge help with this. Two weeks later, Fiona came for the weekend, and that helped enormously also.

I was still struggling with back pain, and I lacked the ability to lift or carry much at a time. The house sale had a very short settlement period, so I had to get packing really quickly. The following week after the house sold, my friend Trisha came over and, with the exception of the pantry, practically packed the whole kitchen for me. I only taped the boxes together and labelled them. I was *so* grateful!

That afternoon, I took the dogs in to visit Geoffrey. He loved it when I brought the dogs in to see him. Instead of sitting on the balcony or in his comfy chair in his room, however, he was lying in his bed using oxygen. It was unexpected, and I was a bit startled that he said that he just felt lousy. The dogs jumped up and lay on him. They stayed there the whole time I stayed, which was strange.

Geoffrey insisted on going to the dining room for dinner, but I discovered the next day that he'd had to be wheelchaired back to his room, as he was too unstable to walk. The following day, he felt no better, although he was sitting in a chair when I arrived in the late morning. I watched as he struggled to eat his lunch in his room. He ate very little.

———◦❖◦———

Over the weekend, although I was spending time packing, I spent as much time with Geoffrey as I could. He seemed to be deteriorating, but he was still able to hold a conversation so long as I was patient while he got his words out.

By Monday, he needed help to eat, so I'd go in twice a day to feed him. We chatted a bit, laughed a bit, and he slept a bit also. That evening, the geriatrician came and ensured that everything was in place to keep Geoffrey as comfortable as possible, as we weren't at all sure that he was going to recover this time.

On the Tuesday evening, Geoffrey asked me to sing to him. I sat close and sang "Annie's Song" by John Denver. He dozed off with a smile on his face.

On Wednesday, he said, "I'm dying, aren't I?"

I didn't know what to say. I felt bad, but I just asked him if that's what it felt like. He said that it did—and that he'd had enough and was ready to go. I told him that he was free to go if he'd had enough of being in a failing body. He also said that he didn't want to leave me and he wondered how I'd manage without him.

I immediately burst out laughing and said, "Honey, I've been looking after you and managing everything on my own for years now." I patted his chest lovingly as I chuckled.

He grinned, giggled, and said, "Oh yeah," acknowledging this truth. Then he immediately fell asleep with a smile on his face.

That evening, he told me that "they won't let me into heaven yet". I wondered what was stopping his passing.

On the Thursday and Friday, I continued to ensure I was there to feed him what little he wanted to eat. I knew the nurses would have fed him, but towards the end of the week, I was only getting grunts or slight nods, and I wanted to be the one to do these last things for him.

My son, Mick, came up from Melbourne on the Friday evening. We had arranged that he would come up for the weekend only a couple of weeks prior because the moving truck was coming the following Thursday, and I could clearly see that I was not going to be able to pack everything in time. It was the bending, lifting, and carrying that was difficult for me, so Mick worked like a Trojan, and once again, I could not have been more grateful.

We visited Geoffrey twice on the Saturday. At lunchtime, he was very woozy and was in and out of consciousness. He still wanted to each a little lunch, but it was hard work for him, and he was falling asleep with food in his mouth. I was having to wake him to remind him to swallow. He struggled to suck a drink from the straw, and Mick made a joke about Geoffrey losing his sucker. This elicited a slight grin from him.

I tried to lift the glass to Geoffrey's lips, but that made him choke. I joked with him about the fact that "Oh dear, it looked like I was trying to kill you". He did have a little giggle over this, but he kept his eyes closed.

He fell asleep, and I cleaned his face. I told him again that I loved him and that many people loved him. I told him I would return later to see if he wanted any dinner, and I'd be there to help.

When we returned at dinner time, there was no dinner for Geoffrey. He was unconscious and unresponsive. We stayed for about an hour and a half, and I told him that I loved him forever, and that he should go to heaven and be peaceful. I'd be perfectly fine. I stroked and kissed his hands and his head, and I thanked him for being a wonderful husband and for looking out for me for all the years that he was able to do so. I told him that I would miss him and reiterated that I'd be OK.

"Always remember that I love you *all the numbers*, my darling," I told him.

Mick and I both hugged him and stroked his head before we left. He passed away peacefully around 5.20 the next morning. It was fifteen days after his eighty-eighth birthday.

———————◆◆◆———————

During the whole process of looking after Geoffrey during his heart condition and his dementia, I found that I continually struggled to allow support for myself. I struggled to be less critical of myself and of others. I struggled to be patient—continually and constantly patient. I struggled to remain happy with myself and my life.

I struggled initially with having to make all the decisions by myself. I struggled with the grief of losing someone who was there but not emotionally available to me anymore. I struggled with the physical demands of my situation. I struggled to not feel trapped. I struggled with not wanting to fail or to give up. The struggles were real, enduring, and deep. They have left scars but have also created reinvigoration.

I have most definitely come out of this a better person, and I thank Geoffrey for that. I must thank my friends, my family, and my soul family, for I could not have braved the journey without their physical, mental, and emotional support. I like to think that I am less critical, more patient, more understanding, more balanced, and happier as a result of the whole experience. I am eternally grateful for everything and everyone as I move into the next chapter of my life.

REFERENCE INFORMATION

Alzheimers Australia
(now Dementia Australia)
www.dementia.org.au
Phone 1800 100 500

National Dementia Helpline
Phone 1800 100 500

Oz Care
www.ozcare.org.au
Phone 1800 692 273

Blue Care
www.bluecare.org.au
Phone 1300 258 322

Beyond Blue
www.beyondblue.org.au
Phone 1300 224 636

My Aged Care
www.myagedcare.gov.au
Phone 1800 200 422

Inner Child Healing Audio or e-book
www.tikashi.com.au/product/inner-child-healing/

Printed in the United States
By Bookmasters